What I Saw in

Heaven

T0103414

What I Saw in Heaven

THE INCREDIBLE TRUE STORY
OF THE DAY I DIED, MET JESUS,
AND RETURNED TO LIFE A NEW PERSON

HEIDI BARR

BakerBooks

a division of Baker Publishing Group
Grand Rapids, Michigan

© 2024 by Heidi Barr

Published by Baker Books
a division of Baker Publishing Group
PO Box 6287, Grand Rapids, MI 49516-6287
BakerBooks.com

Printed in the United States of America

All rights reserved. No part of this publication may be reproduced, stored in a retrieval system, or transmitted in any form or by any means—for example, electronic, photocopy, recording—without the prior written permission of the publisher. The only exception is brief quotations in printed reviews.

Library of Congress Cataloging-in-Publication Data
Names: Barr, Heidi, 1955– author.
Title: What I saw in heaven : the incredible true story of the day I died, met Jesus, and returned to life a new person / Heidi Barr.
Description: Grand Rapids, Michigan : Baker Books, a division of Baker Publishing Group, [2024]
Identifiers: LCCN 2023029527 | ISBN 9781540904126 (paper) | ISBN 9781540904164 (cloth) | ISBN 9781493445721 (ebook)
Subjects: LCSH: Jesus Christ (Spirit) | Heaven.
Classification: LCC BF1311.J5 B67 2024 | DDC 133.9/3—dc23/eng/20231011
LC record available at https://lccn.loc.gov/2023029527

Scripture quotations are from the New Revised Standard Version Updated Edition. Copyright © 2021 National Council of Churches of Christ in the United States of America. Used by permission. All rights reserved worldwide.

Some names and identifying details have been changed to protect the privacy of individuals.

Cover design by Laura Powell

Baker Publishing Group publications use paper produced from sustainable forestry practices and postconsumer waste whenever possible.

24 25 26 27 28 29 30   7 6 5 4 3 2 1

This book is dedicated to my mother.
Good, bad, indifferent—she was my mother,
and in her own way she loved me.
She's with the angels. I miss her.

Contents

Foreword

It was March 2016, and I had just been interviewed on a major New York network news program about my book *Imagine Heaven: Near-Death Experiences, God's Promises, and the Exhilarating Future That Awaits You*. I had researched well over one thousand cases of near-death experiences (NDEs). On the show, I explained how the commonalities I found from cases around the world point to the expectation of heaven we see in the Bible. That night I got this email from a nurse in California:

> I've never before heard of you or your book. I'm Jewish, a registered nurse. I was raised by an atheist and an agnostic, yet at the age of 16 I died and experienced a full-blown NDE. I'm a weird Jew. Don't attend the synagogue. Absolutely believe in God, and I know the person with me during my NDE was Jesus or Yeshua. Very strange. Thanks for your time.
>
> Heidi

Wow! I immediately emailed Heidi back, wanting to hear more of her fascinating story. I was curious: How did she know he was Jesus, and why Jesus if she was raised Jewish with atheist parents? Heidi and I began emailing and talking about her experience, which is one of the most intriguing and evidential ones I've heard.

Heidi's experience of God and of the life to come is not at all what she would have expected, yet it aligns with the thousands of accounts I've studied, and it confirms God's identity as revealed to the Jewish prophets and through Jesus. Heidi came face-to-face with the love, compassion, forgiveness, and inexpressible joy of God. Her story reveals both expected and unexpected aspects of God's winsome character. Like the fact that a sixteen-year-old girl who loved racing across an open meadow bareback on a horse would say that Jesus took her on the wildest ride of her life—more fun than she's ever had.

But Heidi's amazing story is about much more than her heavenly journey. It's about life, family struggles, and redemption by God's amazing guidance and grace. Heidi has been through hell on earth, yet through the many trials and tribulations, she came out the other side a better person. Her story intersects with so many stories of people who have been abused, betrayed, or just beaten up by an evil world and wonder, *Where is God? Is he there? Does he even care?* If you've ever asked those questions or struggled with the evils of this world, Heidi's story will give you hope and a new perspective that will help you to overcome, just as she learned to do. This is a story of life's harsh realities overtaken by heaven's brilliant love and redemption.

Over the past eight years, Heidi has become a good friend to me and my wife, Kathy. I've had many conversations with her since that first email in 2016. I've interviewed her multiple times about her story, and I can tell you, she's the real deal. She's an honest, kind, unpretentious person who loves God and has dedicated her life to serving others as a hospice nurse. She's Jewish, yet she believes in Jesus as her Lord and Messiah because she met him face-to-face when she died. I find it amazing that as a sixteen-year-old with no understanding of God's nature, she describes meeting the triune God of the Bible.

After her hospitalization, Heidi kept her near-death experience to herself. This is common, as the experience is sacred and hard to describe. Imagine trying to describe a three-dimensional world of color to two-dimensional people living in a black-and-white world. That's what I'm convinced people having NDEs are forced to do. They say their experience was more real than this world because it was an experience of more dimensions, sights, sounds, and senses than we have on planet earth. As Heidi wrote to me in a later email,

> I saw flowers and grass—the most vibrant colors—colors we can't even imagine. All were lit from within, glowing with life. And it struck me at the time that even on the most beautiful day here on earth, what we see is a mere reflection of what exists in heaven.

Heidi also had a lot to lose by talking about her near-death experience. Writing about meeting Jesus could mean losing many of her family members and longtime friends.

She has no reason, no motive, to publish this wild story other than that it's true, and she knows God wants her to tell others the truth about him! I'm so glad she has finally published her story because I know it will be a catalyst that God uses to change many lives. It has changed my life for the better, and I'm confident it will do the same for you.

John Burke, pastor and *New York Times* bestselling author of *Imagine Heaven* and *Imagine the God of Heaven*

1

The Accident

I remember many things about the day I died.

My sixteenth birthday had come and gone. I now had my driver's license. It was a weekday, but for some reason, we were out of school. Was it Easter? A teacher's workshop day? I honestly can't pinpoint the date. I know it was before Shavuot, the giving of the Torah—or, as it's known to Christians, Pentecost.

What I do remember is that it was a good day to ride my horse. No rain had been forecast. The weather was decent, the day reasonably warm, partly cloudy. Warmer days were on the way, but we had yet to feel the humidity of an Iowa summer. That would arrive soon, but not today. The wind blew large, fluffy white clouds across a deep blue April sky. All was calm, which was a little unusual in my life. For once, I expected the day to be drama free.

I anticipated nothing out of the ordinary, nothing but a fun, old-fashioned ride on my horse at Shady Lane Ranch. Since my sisters wanted to come as well, and my mother had no plans, she was quite willing to let me borrow the big green 1968 Oldsmobile Delta 88.

Usually on days like this, I would ride with my friend Meryl. Her father had bought her a horse after I'd gotten mine. He'd hoped caring for a horse would be a good outlet for Meryl. She hung out with the same crowd I did, and we'd both had some issues with drugs. She'd experimented a lot more than me, but we never used drugs when we were riding. (At least, I never did.) That day, Meryl was sick with a bad cold, so she declined my offer of a lift out to the ranch. No big deal. Riding by myself was just fine.

As I led my quarter horse, Heather, in from the paddock, I couldn't help but overhear a loud argument in the barn. A woman who owned a gray Arabian mare was arguing with her husband about whether he could ride the horse. I very much doubted he could. The Arabian was ill-behaved under the best of circumstances, and the woman had always had a difficult time controlling her. She'd managed so far, but I wasn't a fan of the mare, and I tended to avoid the pair when they were out on the narrow, thickly forested trails.

Much of the time, Meryl and I rode off the ranch, taking the backcountry roads to Big Lake Park, where we would spend hours swimming with our horses. Or we'd ride a few miles along the side of the county highway, back into Council Bluffs, to buy our horses ice cream cones at one of the local hangouts, Christy Creme Drive-In. We'd ride our horses right up to the window to order. Heather loved vanilla soft-serve ice cream. She especially liked to crunch the cone after she'd licked all the ice cream out of it.

This day, since my sisters had come with me and were waiting, and I was riding alone, I was content to stay on the ranch proper. Charlie, the owner of Shady Lane Ranch, owned several hundred oak tree–covered acres set back into the hills of Pottawattamie County. The ranch itself is still open. I don't know who owns it now. Perhaps Charlie is still alive or his son has kept it going.

I ignored the argument and led Heather through the barn to the hitching post outside, where I brushed her and put on her hackamore. I kept her halter on and knotted the lead rope around her neck. Since I didn't have a saddle and I wasn't the best jumper, I used the fence as a mounting block to climb onto her back. I headed off into the hills, leaving my sisters behind.

Both of my sisters liked to hang out at the ranch. Shady Lane was a fun place. Usually everyone was relaxed and happy. But then, hanging out with horses tends to make one relaxed and happy. My youngest sister often played with the miniature horses, a paint mare and her white colt. Although my middle sister loved horses, she was allergic to them, so when I rode off, she remained in the Oldsmobile.

I headed up the main trail and disappeared into my own private world for an hour, communing with Heather, communing with nature, and enjoying the day. I saw no one else on my ride aside from the bright red cardinals—my favorite bird—darting from tree to tree, the squawking blue jays, the diligent robins on the hunt for worms, and the black squirrels native to that part of Iowa. This was the best, the one thing I loved—to be alone with my horse.

I felt at peace.

I felt so peaceful that although I knew my sisters were probably getting bored, I didn't rush back. Heather and I made our way toward the trail down to the barn, but I turned off to the side so I could sit on her back a little longer. I was reluctant to leave her and return home. Heather calmed me. Being on her back, the rhythm of riding, gave me both a sense of peace and a feeling of exhilaration. Nothing compared to the joy I experienced on the back of a horse, especially when Heather and I were galloping full speed across an open meadow.

I was perhaps a few hundred yards from the side of the barn, sitting quietly on my horse, when I saw my sisters farther down the hill. My middle sister appeared to be reading in the car. My youngest sister stood near the miniature horses, petting the young colt. When I heard pounding hoofbeats coming from farther up the trail, I knew immediately who it was and what that meant. The man had won the argument. He'd taken out the ill-tempered Arabian mare, and now he was out of control—she was racing at breakneck speed toward the barn.

Every stable I've been associated with has many safety rules, including no running back to the barn. It makes for barn-sour horses and dangerous situations. Charlie had that hard-and-fast rule at Shady Lane, but in this case, it was meaningless.

I didn't have a whole lot of time to react, and I didn't know what to do. I had nowhere to go, no way to get my horse clear. Heather and I were at the end of a trail. We stood essentially at a dead end. Moving would put me directly in the man's path.

The hoofbeats grew louder. The horse was getting closer. I could see them now, the Arabian and the man flapping on her back. He'd dropped the reins and had a death grip on the saddle horn.

I had the presence of mind to think, *I hope she doesn't step on her reins. She'll flip and dump the man, and they might both get badly injured.*

My next thought was about myself. *Okay, if I stay on Heather, the mare will see her standing still and she'll calm down.*

But she didn't. She kept coming.

Okay, she'll avoid me and make her way to the barn.

But she didn't. She came right at us.

Maybe I should dismount. But I was concerned I would be injured if both horses got tangled up.

Heather began to get nervous; she danced around. I attempted to keep her calm and under control, but we had very little room to maneuver, no place to get out of the way.

Still that horse kept coming. In hindsight, I should have dismounted and let Heather go, but my thoughts were a jumble. I was afraid the Arabian mare would trample me. It was a very real possibility. I reasoned I might be safer on Heather's back.

That Arabian galloped right at us. She barely missed us, almost clipping us as she raced past. I was aware enough to know she came within an inch or two of Heather's rump.

At that moment Heather reared up. I dropped the reins, leaned forward, and grabbed her chestnut mane, gripping it with both hands. Heather came back down, then reared up again. This time either one or both of her back feet slid off the narrow, sloping trail. She flipped over backward, falling downhill and across my body, crushing me.

The instant Heather's back fell across my chest, I died.

2

What I Saw in Heaven

I left my body and found myself up in the air, perhaps thirty or forty feet above the scene. I looked down and watched as Heather rolled over me. My lifeless, skinny teenage body was tossed like a rag doll. I prayed in that moment that Heather wouldn't get injured. She righted herself, slid down the hill, and ran toward the barn. I was relieved to see she seemed to be fine.

I saw and heard my little sister scream. She covered her eyes with her hands. My middle sister pressed her face against the car window.

I watched as the man and the Arabian galloped into the barn. Heather followed. Chaos ensued as people, Charlie, the man's wife, and other riders with their horses scattered and scrambled to get out of the way. Charlie's black stallion, locked in his stall, threw an absolute fit, screeching, rearing, and kicking at the door.

I found it interesting that I could see through the timbers and the rusted metal shingles directly into the old, weathered gray barn. The open door faced away from me, yet I could see everything happening inside the barn, as if the roof had somehow vanished into thin air.

As I floated there, just watching, I realized I didn't care about me, about the dead body lying in the dirt. That body mattered not a whit. It was nothing but a shell built to house my soul. It meant nothing to me. I knew I was dead, absolutely. That was a simple fact, and it didn't trouble me.

My only concern was for my young sisters. My middle sister was fourteen years old. My youngest sister was only eleven. They seemed to be frozen in place, horrified by what was happening, terror obvious on their faces. I was so sad for them. My heart broke because they witnessed my traumatic death. It was something from which they might never recover.

"I wish my sisters didn't have to see me die," I said.

The moment I spoke those words, I became aware of a light that was sort of flowing over my right shoulder. It was a golden light, bathing everything before me in a golden hue, lighting up the entire scene. I knew it wasn't the sun, which was behind some clouds. Besides, the sun would have been shining overhead, not over my right shoulder.

I turned to look, and I saw a man floating with me in the air. I stared at his face. He smiled and I smiled back. He moved forward until he floated right by my side.

I recognized him immediately. How could I not? This was the man I'd done my best to ignore for four long years. And here he was, grinning from ear to ear.

How do we speak when we're dead? I don't remember my mouth moving, but I remember saying, "Hi! I know you!" I knew him better than I knew my own name.

This was Jesus. There was no doubt in my mind. This man was, without question, Jesus, Yeshua. Because of my father's atheism and his disdain for all things religious, especially Christianity, Jesus was the name I'd never been allowed to utter in my home, at least not in a way that acknowledged him as anything other than a hoax.

At the sight of his face, I felt my heart overflow with happiness. He grinned at me, every bit as happy as I was. Happier, because he is all joy and happiness.

So much occurred at once. I wish I had the right words to explain my journey with Jesus, my experience with him, but I don't. There aren't enough words in any language to explain Jesus, God, the Holy Spirit, or heaven, so please be patient. I will try my best to tell this story in a coherent fashion.

There we were, Jesus and I, up in the air. All things became peripheral to him. I knew things were taking place on the ground, but I no longer paid attention. Just as my dead body was immaterial, those things occurring below us became immaterial the instant I saw his face.

I was once again the child I'd been when he would wrap me up in his light, soft as a cloud, and rock me to sleep. I felt the same as I did back then—safe, understood, accepted, surrounded by his loving presence.

Jesus was all at once my father, my brother, and my best friend. He was everything to me.

In that eternal moment, I didn't think of any of the bad stuff that had happened to me. My mind and my heart and my soul were focused on him and on how much he loved me. He loved me freely. He loved me for no reason.

I certainly didn't deserve his love. I hadn't prayed to Jesus. Ever.

Yet here he was.

Jesus and I had all the time in the world. Either time wasn't a factor because after you die there is no time, or after you die you have all the time in the world. Regardless, every moment felt like, or was, an eternity.

While we were still above my body, Jesus held out his right hand and a three-dimensional movie of my life began to play. But rather than the story of my life progressing from start to finish in chronological order, I saw my life all at once, from the moment of conception to the present day.

He had been right beside me.

He had formed me in my mother's womb.

He had sat beside me, chatted with me, when I was an infant in my playpen. I saw him there again, teaching me.

As we watched the story of my life, he paused at a silly scene. I was an infant of four or five months and could already sit up. I was in my playpen, shaking a pink plastic telephone rattle. Jesus sat right next to me, leaning close to speak to me. And I was listening to him and shaking my rattle. There was a knock at the door and my mother went to open it. I watched, both through my baby eyes and my sixteen-year-old eyes, as a couple entered. The woman carried a baby who was near my age. I recognized him. I'd met this baby before.

His mother set him down right in the playpen, right where Jesus was sitting. The first thing that baby did was grab the rattle from my hand and use it to whack me over the bridge of my nose. I screamed until my mother came and lifted me out of the playpen. I wasn't hurt, but my baby face was beet red with anger and indignation.

Watching this, Jesus and I burst out laughing. I could see that he'd laughed even when it happened. He and I floated side by side in the air, laughing our heads off.

Remarkable, isn't it? Can you imagine what it's like to watch a life review with Jesus and see Jesus with you as a child?

Jesus stopped the tape again and again to show me how I'd affected others. If I'd been kind, I could feel the reaction to my kindness, as if I had been the recipient of the act. In other words, I could feel what the other person felt. I'd been a pretty good kid. For the most part, I'd been kind and considerate to others, regardless of how I'd been treated. Jesus didn't even seem to consider the fights I'd had with my parents to be anything out of the ordinary. He dismissed those entirely.

But I'd deliberately committed one cruel act. When I was ten years old, my father was driving me and a thirteen-year-old boy to Hebrew school. I was tall for my age, and this boy was very small for his age. Sitting in the back seat of the car, I turned to him and said with an extremely snarky tone, "Why are you so shrimpy?"

What an awful, hurtful thing to say.

I'd immediately felt bad when I'd said it, but I shrugged it off. Now Jesus showed me the impact my words had upon this boy.

When I heard myself say those words, I felt his heart shrink in his chest. I felt his pain. I understood that he still carried the pain I had inflicted. I knew right then and there that everything we do, every word we say, has an impact on others. We can hurt people with words alone. We can crush another's heart and soul.

But Jesus didn't judge me or condemn me. He stayed right beside me, comforting me, reassuring me, as I judged and condemned myself.

I felt horrible about how I'd hurt that boy. I didn't want to behave like that ever again.

In hindsight, I find it interesting that the life review didn't focus on what had been done *to* me. It was all about my actions. How had I treated others? That was Jesus' number one question for me. How had I lived my life, spent my time here on earth?

The hurt and the pain I'd experienced at the hands of others weren't even there. It was as if none of it had happened. It wasn't my hurt or my pain to carry. I may have sinned, but the abuse I experienced wasn't my sin.

Jesus had been right beside me through all the pain and struggles in my life. He'd suffered and struggled along with me. I had never, not for a single second, been alone.

In my life review, Jesus didn't scold me, even as he pointed out my mistakes and missteps. He's not a scolder. He's not a nag. He doesn't wag his finger. Not once did he say, "Quit smoking. Stop using drugs. Stop hanging out with those kids." He didn't say anything about all the ways I was hurting myself. There were many things he communicated to me; Jesus communicates very clearly. But he doesn't nag.

When I tell my story, I always say there was no breast-beating, there was no finger-pointing, there was no condemnation. There was only love. Jesus *is* love.

Before Jesus and I left the barn, the scene of the accident, and my dead body, I became aware of something else. I had no more questions. All my nagging existential questions had vanished. They'd been answered. Why are we here? What is the meaning of life? Is there a God? What is humanity? What happens after we die?

These weren't things I'd even thought about. I hadn't asked any questions; I simply became aware that I knew the answers.

Of course, if you ask me what those answers are, I can't tell you. I remember some things, but the moment I came back to life, I realized this: When I was dead, I'd known all the answers. Once I was alive again, I only knew that I'd known the answers, and that made perfect sense.

If we had all the answers and were aware of the details about our lives, the directions our lives would take, there would be no point in living the life God has planned for each one of us. Why would we? We'd already know everything we wanted to know, and we would sit around and essentially twiddle our thumbs. Life would be meaningless. We would each be our own little god, so to speak. Certainly, we'd have no need of God. Therefore, I'd rather not know everything. Forgetting seemed right and proper to me.

It's in seeking God that we become truly humble, truly human. We each become the person he intends us to be, the person he created us to be.

It's in seeking and suffering that we turn to God, although perhaps many sufferers turn away. How I wish we could avoid the suffering part. Unfortunately, I don't believe that's possible in this life.

In that moment with Jesus, did I ask him to change my life? Undo all the bad stuff I had experienced, undo the suffering? No. It never occurred to me to ask him to change a thing. The bad was forgotten. I was surrounded with his love, washed clean by it. My soul was healed, mended by his love.

Nothing else mattered.

3

Surfing with Jesus on a Wave of Light

Jesus took my hand, and off we flew. We left the scene of my death.

It wasn't quite flying, although I did stretch out my left arm like a bird's wing. What we did was surf. Jesus took me bodysurfing on a wave of light. It was so much better than riding my horse.

I looked down and saw a wave of light like an ocean wave, rolling beneath our bare feet, pushing us forward, faster and faster. The light was made of all colors. I laughed as it tickled the bottoms of my feet. As I stretched out my arm, the light flowed through my fingers like water.

Jesus said, "This is so cool!"

And it was. I could not have agreed more. This was the coolest thing ever in the history of the world!

Jesus and I laughed out loud. His smile was so wide, and there was such a mischievous sparkle in his eyes. His sense of fun was contagious. He loved gifting this experience to me and sharing it with me. I was awed by his power, his laughter, and his joy as we journeyed together.

We passed over fields of corn and soybeans. We must have headed west because I remember crossing the Missouri River. We passed over houses, cities, small towns, creeks, rivers, rolling hills, and mountains. But aside from a deliberate glance or two at the wave of light surging beneath our feet, my focus was on Jesus' face. I didn't want to miss out on any of the joy and laughter and love flowing from his eyes, so anything I was able to see, I saw as we passed by. In other words, I caught only a passing glimpse of things beyond his shoulders and head.

We passed places on earth, but Jesus and I were traveling very fast, and soon I no longer saw anything of earth. It seemed that we had left this beautiful blue planet behind, but I wasn't entirely sure what else I was seeing. Planets? Stars? A galaxy? I didn't really care. Jesus was all that mattered to me.

It hit me later that we had passed the moon, and I could see Mercury, Venus, and Mars. We saw Jupiter with its great red eye. We surfed by beautiful golden Saturn and its rings. Saturn was so pretty! We saw lovely, lonely ice-blue Neptune and its moons.

We traveled farther into space, passing a double star, and then together we gazed at the amazing Helix Nebula. We passed a spiral galaxy, and I knew exactly which one it was—the Andromeda Galaxy. Awestruck and, quite frankly, almost overwhelmed, I thought, *This is what God sees when he wakes up in the morning.*

Jesus smiled at me. He was so pleased I'd recognized God's immensity. Believe me, that immensity will bring us to our knees. Our brains can't grasp the reality of the Father without tripping our mental circuit breaker. The Israelites were right to tremble at Mount Sinai (Exod. 19:16).

Jesus and I traveled faster and faster. The ride was exhilarating. Fantastic. Incredible. As we surfed, I discerned a few individual things, but ultimately, we reached a point where we were going so fast there was no more individuation. Jesus and I were individuals, and I could still see him and feel the warmth of his hand clasping mine, but all around us there was only One Thing.

I knew that One Thing was God.

The simplest way I can describe this is to say that there's no corner, no place, no space that God doesn't occupy. He contains everything, and everything is contained in him. He is in us. We are in him.

What I experienced is difficult to express in words. John's Gospel says this much better than I can, and even though the sentence is very simple, its meaning is still a bit perplexing because God's immanence is hard for our small minds to grasp: "On that day you will know that I am in my Father, and you in me, and I in you" (John 14:20).

Jesus was in the Father and in me, and I was in him. I wish I could explain this better, but God is beyond words. He was one, and he was himself, but he was in me too. There was a part of him in me. There really aren't any

words to describe this awareness. Knowing and understanding it was simple when I was dead. When I came back
to life, I had no way to properly and accurately explain
God's oneness. He may be Three, but he is One.

At that moment, Jesus and I approached a threshold.
I don't know if it was exactly a threshold, but that's the
only way I can describe it. Imagine approaching a large
doorway, then passing through it. That's essentially what
we did.

As we crossed the threshold, I saw a light.

I'm taking a deep breath now because, again, finding
the right words to describe this event is so challenging! I
hope and pray I can do justice to the moment. As I've said,
there's a reason I can't remember everything. God allows
me to remember enough to give hope, but no more than
that. I'm reminded of Paul, who said,

> I know a person in Christ who fourteen years ago was
> caught up to the third heaven—whether in the body or out
> of the body I do not know; God knows. And I know that
> such a person—whether in the body or out of the body I
> do not know; God knows—was caught up into paradise
> and heard things that are not to be told, that no mortal
> is permitted to repeat. (2 Cor. 12:2–4)

The light beyond the threshold took up my entire field
of vision. It was a perfect, white, blemish-less light, and it
was infinite in scope. There was no end to it, no beginning.
The light was alive, and the light was love.

Jesus guided me directly into the light, and I found
myself sitting on God's lap. God the Father, yes, but Jesus

too. They were one and the same yet separate, but again, still one.

See how difficult this is to explain?

So there I was, sitting on God's lap, kicking my legs like a little girl. I had my arms wrapped around his waist. I buried my face in his chest. Talk about a perfect love. Love incarnate. All love. Every single smidge of love in existence. That was God.

He had his arms around me too. He held me tight. And he's a big God. I was like a toddler sitting on her father's lap. How God can have a body, I don't know, but he can if he so chooses. God can do anything.

I had a sense I shouldn't look at his face—certainly not in the way I'd had my eyes glued to Jesus' face. I snuck a quick glance upward and then just as quickly buried my head against God's chest. I couldn't see his face. It seemed to be shrouded in clouds, obscured somehow. And I think that was a good thing. I don't think any human can or should see his face. Moses spoke with God face-to-face—in Hebrew, *peh ah peh*, or mouth-to-mouth—and he had to wear a veil so the light shining from his face didn't frighten the Israelites.

I wasn't troubled by the fact that I couldn't see God the Father's face. I was humbled, but I felt no fear, only awe in the truest sense of the word.

I had come home to my real Father. He loved me. He loved me with all the love in the universe.

What my dad had told me wasn't true. It was a lie. My life was not less significant than the most microscopic speck of dust in the universe. My life had significance to God.

31

God knew me. God comforted me. God accepted me. God loved me.

God filled every single corner of me. He filled my heart. I never wanted to leave him.

If someone had asked me, "Would you like to remain here on God's lap forever?" I would have replied, "Yes, thank you." And I'd have happily, gratefully kept my face buried in his chest for all eternity.

That was what these moments felt like to me—an eternity with God.

Then God shifted my position in such a way that I lifted my head. He wanted to show me something, so I looked where he indicated.

I will try to explain. Picture an infinite God/light wearing a pure white robe of light, also infinite in size and scope, extending through all space and time. Picture this infinite God/light pulling back the corner of his robe that was infinitely far away. It was only by withdrawing a portion of himself that I was able to see what he wanted to show me.

On earth, in this life, I was nearly blind. My vision was terrible. I'd worn glasses with thick lenses since the second grade. But when I was dead, I had perfect vision. We're not perfect on earth. God perfects us in heaven.

Keep in mind, too, that what God wanted to show me was infinitely far away. Despite my poor vision on earth, now I could see everything as if it were right in front of me. I could see every single detail as if it were mere inches from my face.

The first thing I saw was grass. It was like the grass on earth, and its color was like the green of earth, but it was different as well. This color epitomized green. It was the essence, the source, the heart of green. I realized that all the colors we experience on earth are mere reflections of the colors of heaven, and they pale in comparison. The most beautiful, perfect day on earth, while worthy and worthwhile and lovely, is still a pale reflection of every day in heaven.

That doesn't mean we shouldn't appreciate the beauty God has created for us here. I learned above all that each day is a gift for which we should give thanks. God created this world to be beautiful. He created it for our enjoyment and pleasure. We should take care of each other, and we should take care of his creation.

As I looked at the grass in this infinite-sized meadow, I could have counted each blade, as every single one was so perfect, so precise, and so clear. The most amazing part? The grass was singing! I'll never forget what I saw and heard, what I witnessed. Each blade of grass sang the praises of God.

The music was astonishing, amazing, gorgeous, heavenly, awesome. My eyes were riveted on the grass. I was fascinated. I will never forget the sight of it, but there was more. I saw flowers.

The flowers in heaven looked like flowers on earth. I saw a patch that reminded me of irises, but the blue of the petals was so very blue—a deep, essential, living, true blue—and I could see every dark blue vein in every petal. I could see every part of the plant in detail. I saw many other kinds of flowers of all different colors, but it was the vibrant blue of these that drew my gaze repeatedly. Viewing all these myriad fields of flowers astonished and fascinated me.

I looked farther and saw grove upon grove of trees. Imagine a grove of aspen trees, but bigger, stronger, taller, more vital and alive. I could see every single leaf on every single tree, and I could see every vein on every leaf.

I was infinitely far away, seated on God's lap. How could I see such details? I don't know. This was God's doing. And it was marvelous in my new eyes.

As I listened to the grass singing, as I watched the irises swaying and the leaves on the aspen trees quaking, I realized there was no wind. The flowers and the trees were swaying in time to the song of the grass, and all were moving in the light of God. God's light flowed through everything, animating everything. It gave life to everything I saw.

As I watched this remarkable sight, I noticed a path through the bright green grass. It wound through the flower-filled meadow and past the trees, becoming wider as it moved up a low, rounded, grass-covered hill. I heard people singing. They, too, were singing the praises of God. Now I could see them—figures coming toward me on the path, their voices filled with joy—but I couldn't quite make out their faces yet. It was as if there was a veil between us. I thought I would meet these people.

4

Return from Heaven

Jesus stood beside me again. He took my hand in his. He seemed serious, concerned. "You didn't die," he said. "You have to go back."

I understood that he was saying I hadn't died permanently. But I pulled my hand from his, wrapped my arms around God's waist, and buried my face in God's chest. "I'm not going back."

Jesus again took my hand. "You didn't die," he said again. "You have to go back."

I looked at him and shook my head. "No, I'm not going back."

God released his hold on me, making it clear he agreed with Jesus.

Jesus tugged my hand, pulling me right off God's lap. He and I stood, facing each other. His voice was stern. "You didn't die. You have to go back."

"No!" Now I was yelling. "I'm not going back! I'm not going back! I'll feel pain!" I tried to pull my hand from his. I may have been in heaven, but I was still a teenager.

Despite my protestations, Jesus took me back. You don't argue with Jesus.

Do you recall all those times in the Bible when God "remembers" his promises to Israel? I got the distinct feeling that I was supposed to die that day, but God "remembered" a promise I'd made to him years before. He "remembered" my purpose and destiny on earth.

This time there was no surfing, no colorful, exciting wave of light. Jesus and I were—*bam!*—right above my lifeless body. I looked down at myself and wondered how on earth I would get into that body. I sure didn't want to. No way.

Charlie, the ranch owner, knelt beside my dead body, crying, praying. My sisters were crying. Aside from that, everyone and everything at the ranch was silent, watching, waiting. Even my horse, Heather, stood all by herself behind Charlie, perfectly still.

Jesus wrapped his arm around my shoulders and shoved me into my body from beneath, from back to front. It was like being vacuumed in. He shoved me in so fast that I hit the inside of my face. I literally hit the inside of my skull. And I panicked. You cannot comprehend just how panic-stricken I was.

The sensation of being trapped was terrifying. I struggled inside my body. My dead body didn't move, but the body Jesus had just shoved inside fought to get back out. It was the most claustrophobic feeling imaginable.

Suddenly, Jesus was in my body with me. We both fit in there. When it comes to Jesus, he can do anything. For lack of a better word, he smoothed my arms into my arms and my legs into my legs. He again made me whole, one person.

I was now in my body, but I couldn't remember how to do anything. I had no idea how my body worked, and it seemed to take me forever to remember. At long last I managed to crack open one eye. I inhaled. I croaked out, "Charlie . . ."

He let out a yelp and shouted, "Thank God! Thank God!"

In a total panic, he proceeded to do the worst thing someone could do under the circumstances. He threw me over my horse. He'd jumped onto her back when she'd arrived in the barn without me, and he'd ridden out to find me. Now he threw me into the back seat of the car, gathered up my sisters, and drove right past the hospital to my house. He carried me upstairs to my bed and told my mother I'd been in an accident. If he said anything else to her, I didn't hear it.

My mother left me under the supervision of my eleven-year-old sister, weak, in shock, unable to move, while she drove Charlie back out to his ranch.

If I had to guess how long I'd been dead, I would say somewhere between four and six minutes. I can only estimate based on how long it might have taken Charlie, who was in the barn dealing with the chaos caused by the runaway Arabian mare, to realize something else was amiss. He would have had to get Heather under control, climb onto her back, ride out to find me, jump off my horse, and kneel down by my side.

I don't know if he told my mother any of these things. I don't know if he described the accident to her or if he was too afraid to tell her the truth. I didn't see Charlie again because while I was still recovering, my father bought some property out in the country and arranged for Charlie to move Heather out there. Shortly after the move, my parents sold her.

My mother returned home from Charlie's ranch and slid an electric heating pad under my lower back. Then she went downstairs to finish making supper. At one point she called up to me and asked if I was coming down for supper. I looked at my little sister and shook my head. I couldn't move. I could barely speak, let alone eat supper.

Aside from my youngest sister, with whom I shared a bedroom, I was left alone all night. I couldn't feel anything, so I didn't realize the heating pad my mother had slid beneath me was burning me. I sustained a serious burn in one spot that later became a decubitus ulcer, or bedsore, when I was stuck flat on my back in the hospital.

In the immediate aftermath of my accident, I couldn't walk. I couldn't feel any sensation on my skin from the waist down, although I suffered terrible pain in my back, legs, hips, and chest. It hurt to breathe. I was very much in shock. But all I could think about was Jesus. All I could see was his face. I honestly didn't think about the state of my broken body.

I felt the pain. I knew I'd been seriously injured. But still I thought of Jesus and God and what had happened.

I told my little sister about meeting Jesus and God, about heaven, and she believed. She'd seen me die. She'd seen my lifeless body. She believed me. But I didn't have the strength to tell anyone else that day.

It wasn't until the next day, after taking my sisters to school, that my mother came to check on me. She realized I still couldn't walk, that I was, in fact, in shock. She finally noticed I hadn't been able to urinate. It was then she decided to drive me to the medical clinic where our neighbor Dr. Carson worked.

I wish I could tell you that my mother had called an ambulance or asked someone—anyone—for help, but she didn't. I was forced to use my arms to drag my useless lower body down a flight of stairs. I dragged myself out the front door, across the cement porch, down the uneven, cracked porch steps, and along the sidewalk to the car. I pulled myself into the back seat, where I lay flat on my stomach. All this time I still couldn't feel anything from the waist down.

I should have been worried, very worried. But I wasn't thinking about me. I was thinking about Jesus' beautiful face. I couldn't stop thinking about him.

Jesus was everything. Whatever happened to me would happen. He would still be everything. Honestly, you must think it's strange, but I wasn't worried.

When we arrived at the clinic, my mother did at last go in and ask for help, and I was wheeled in on a gurney. Dr. Carson took many X-rays.

"Mother, she's going straight to the hospital," he said. He looked me in the eye and said, "You will lie flat on your back for the next month, and you will not move. Do you understand?"

I nodded.

He had me transported to the hospital by ambulance.

My recovery wasn't as smooth as he'd hoped, but I did the best I could under the circumstances.

Dr. Carson didn't call in a surgeon or an orthopedist. He didn't consult with a neurologist or a neurosurgeon or a cardiologist. He should have. He didn't have privileges at the hospital where my father sat on the board of directors, so he admitted me to the new hospital instead of transporting me to the well-staffed, well-funded, long-established hospital complete with a trauma center, orthopedists, orthopedic surgeons, neurologists, and neurosurgeons.

This new hospital was understaffed. And that's an understatement. The entire orthopedic floor was staffed by one RN or LVN and one CNA per shift. There simply weren't enough staff to care for all the patients.

Despite everything I went through—and much of my initial recovery was very challenging—I healed, body and soul. I give all credit to God. He was my physician, my miracle worker.

My healing took many months, but I made a complete recovery. I regained the ability to walk without any medical intervention or even physical therapy.

This was God's doing. God is the ultimate physician. His intervention was the only intervention I received.

5

Jackboots on the Stairs

Over the years since the accident I've often wondered, *How could this have happened to me? What led me to the fateful day when I died, met Jesus, and returned to this life?* Let me share the story of my childhood and early teenage years, so you can truly understand the life-altering impact of my unexpected and unlikely journey to heaven and back and my meeting with Jesus.

My first memory as a small child is of God. He was present at my bedside as far back as I can remember. You might think a child can't remember much, but I do. I remember the very first apartment we lived in. It was where we lived when my parents brought me home from the hospital as a newborn. Obviously, I don't recall coming home from the hospital, but I do recall the apartment.

Our apartment was the bottom floor of an old house that had been divided into three apartments. My father's sister and her husband had purchased the house along with my parents so that my mother and father would have a place to live.

My mother worked as a bookkeeper to help put my dad through law school. Once I was born, she became a full-time mom. My father joined a law practice as an associate, but he made very little money. He made a total of fifty dollars in his first year of practice.

In exchange for our rent-free apartment, he managed the apartment house for my aunt and uncle. My grandparents, who owned a corner market and butcher shop, the Madison Avenue Grocery Store, provided all our groceries. To make some extra money, my father also delivered groceries for my grandfather in the evenings and on weekends.

The house opened onto Washington Avenue via a heavy, dark wooden door. To the right of the door was a coat stand. To the left was a green fabric–covered couch that could be converted into a bed. My parents slept there. A chair and table sat near the coat stand. There was a ceiling light in the center of the living room and a floor lamp near the couch.

During the day, my playpen sat beneath the square archway that opened into the dining room. I slept in my playpen in the dining room every night, although my parents had to walk through that room to reach the bathroom and the kitchen.

I remember sitting in my high chair in the kitchen, the brightest room in the apartment. The kitchen had a double window above the sink and another beside the refrigerator, with cheerful yellow curtains tied open on them. During the day, my mother and I spent most of our time in the kitchen. She smiled, laughed, and played games with me and sang songs to me.

When I was a year old, we moved to a three-bedroom, two-bathroom home on Mount Vernon Drive, in a new development in Council Bluffs. Initially, my mother was happy. But once my middle sister was born, when I was two and a half, I don't remember any more singing, smiles, or laughter from her. We played no more games. It's possible my mother suffered from postpartum depression. She also came from a family prone to depression, and my father's emotional issues, demands for support, and constant need for attention didn't help. Her depression was especially pronounced after my youngest sister was born.

I've asked my youngest sister, "Do you remember a time when Mom was happy?"

She said, "No, I never remember a time when Mom was happy."

My mother's laughter was such a rare occurrence that we remember it to the very depths of our souls. When she laughed, the sun broke through the thick dark clouds that seemed to surround our home. Those are some precious memories.

If my mother loved us—and I believe she did—she didn't know how to express her love. It was clear we were a burden. Although my sisters and I shared many experiences, each of us had a different role in the family. I can't speak for them, but the way my mother and father regarded me and treated me contributed to my belief that I was unloved.

Except in the eyes of God. He loved me. I knew this even as a child. My *real Father* loved me. Knowing I had a *real Father* saved my life many times.

Did God sit at my bedside, at the head of my bed? Yes, he did. I clearly remember *knowing* he was there. He was real to me, a tangible person or presence. God wasn't just a feeling. I didn't imagine him. I had a powerful sense that he sat right next to me, listening to my childish hopes and fears and dreams. He paid attention to my complaints when some injustice had been done.

God also rocked me to sleep every single night. In truth, it was Jesus, but I didn't know it at the time. Of course, Jesus and God are one and the same yet different, and that's a concept I'll leave to the theologians and the Christian apologists because it's beyond my limited comprehension.

A great many things scared me as a child—some big, some small. I could get past the small. It was the big things that stood in the way of a restful night's sleep.

Here's how God rocked me to sleep. When I lay in bed, I felt my entire body surrounded by warmth like that of an electric blanket, but this was a soft, living warmth. I know that seems odd, but I experienced God's warmth like being wrapped in a cloud. As it increased and my body began to relax, my bed would sway from side to side. Sometimes, just for fun, God would slowly lift my bed and then lower it, again and again, until I fell asleep.

During my life review with Jesus, I learned it was Jesus who had done this for me. I saw him there exactly as I'd pictured him, sitting at the head of my bed, right beside my pillow, his head inclined toward me as he listened.

When he felt it was time for me to sleep, he himself surrounded me with his own light and rocked me.

I saw Jesus by my side from the moment of my conception. He formed me in my mother's womb. As Psalm 139:13 says,

> For it was you who formed my inward parts;
> you knit me together in my mother's womb.

I didn't read that psalm until a few years after I'd died. In fact, I didn't read the entire Hebrew Bible or any of the New Testament until that time.

My father, like my mother, suffered from depression. He also suffered from severe anxiety. His emotional issues were somewhat like my mother's, but where she seemed to suffer in silence, he suffered out loud. He was driven to share the fear and the stress he felt. He shared it with me every single day. In a sense, my father lived a double life.

My father was always held in high regard in our community. He served on many boards and volunteered his time for many charitable organizations. He was also a natural-born comedian. He was so funny, he could reduce an entire room of people to tears of laughter, and there was nothing he liked more than an audience.

At home, the facade fell away to reveal his inner torment. He was haunted by his own demons. I don't know how this happened. I don't know what went wrong in his life. What I do know is that he was, in a sense, tortured, and because of that, he tortured us—not physically but emotionally. As a child, I pictured my father as a black hole of despair. Nothing would ever fill that hole. He was lonely in his despair, too lonely to keep his pain to himself.

———

When my father put us to bed at night, he made sure to remind us of the Nazis.

Both sides of his family had emigrated to America, settling in Iowa and Nebraska, many years before Hitler came to power in Germany. His father's family came around 1880, and his mother's father arrived around 1897 and then brought his whole family here in 1901. My mother's ancestors came to the States and settled in Nebraska between 1870 and 1880.

The Holocaust made a deep impression on my father and every Jewish person. It's part of our DNA, and for good reason. By the end of World War II, six million Jews were dead. Although we can't know for certain, it's more likely than not that some of our relatives were killed in the Holocaust.

My father had come of age as a Jew in Middle America during World War II. He was a third-generation American, and he experienced little anti-Semitism.

Even though my father had been safe in the Midwest during the war, World War II deeply affected his family. His older brother's bomber was shot down over occupied France, and his brother spent eighteen months in a German POW camp. My father was very close with his oldest

46

brother, and this left an emotional wound from which my father never recovered.

According to him, long before that event he was already terrified of death. Around the age of eight he developed a pathological fear of dying, an unnatural preoccupation with death, especially with sudden death.

My father obsessed about the Nazis. He warned us nightly to listen for jackboots on the stairs. That was how the Nazis came to take away little Jewish children like us—we would hear their jackboots on the stairs. We would be rousted from our beds, forced out of our home at gunpoint, herded to a train station, loaded into a crowded cattle car, and shipped off to a concentration camp. There we would face the selection process, probably supervised by Dr. Josef Mengele himself, the Nazi "angel of death."

Of course, we'd be sent to the gas chamber. All young children went straight to the gas chamber. Unless Dr. Mengele chose us for his gruesome, inhumane medical experiments, which we heard about in detail.

My dad said our neighbors wouldn't lift a finger to help us. In fact, he claimed they would turn us in to the SS. His words both terrified me and galvanized me.

I shared a bedroom with my youngest sister. By the time I was in the second grade, I'd come up with a plan. The instant I heard the pounding of jackboots on the stairs, I'd kick out the screen in the window next to my bed, grab my sister, slide down the sloping roof, and climb onto the closest branch of the huge elm tree beside our house. Then she and I would shimmy down the tree and run across the street to the woods. We'd hide in our secret spot, the meeting place for the older neighborhood kids.

Adults didn't know about it. I prayed the Nazis wouldn't come in the winter, but no matter what, I was determined she and I would survive.

How? I didn't know, but we would survive. And if we didn't? If we froze to death? It was better than going to a gas chamber.

———

It wasn't merely the Nazis and jackboots on the stairs. It was worse than that. I recently asked my youngest sister if she remembered the two words my father said over and over as he read us the associated newspaper articles from the Council Bluffs *Daily Nonpareil*, the *Omaha World-Herald*, and even the *Chicago Tribune*. Two. Words.

She replied without hesitation: "Richard. Speck."

In 1966 Richard Speck brutally killed eight nursing students in Illinois. My father discussed his terrible acts in detail with us, his two young daughters, two of his three children. We didn't understand all the words, but we understood the horror. In my father's estimation, it was never a matter of if, it was only a matter of when. It would happen. It would happen to us. And we would die at the hand of Richard Speck's doppelgänger.

Neither my father nor my mother could protect us from this horror any more than they could protect us from the Nazis. They wouldn't even try. My father shrugged when I asked him if he would help save us from the Nazis, save us from Richard Speck. Our situation felt hopeless.

When I was ten years old, I knew with absolute clarity I'd never do to my children what my parents did to us.

I even swore an oath to God, just like Scarlett O'Hara did in *Gone with the Wind*. After the burning of Atlanta as she desperately made her way back to Tara, driving a broken-down horse pulling a broken-down wagon carrying Melanie and Melanie's infant son, Scarlett found a carrot buried in the mud. They were starving, so Scarlett stuffed the carrot into her mouth as fast as she could, but then she coughed it back up. She held her fist to the sky and uttered these memorable words: "As God is my witness, as God is my witness, they're not going to lick me. I'm going to live through this and when it's over, I'll never be hungry again. No, nor any of my folk. If I have to lie, steal, cheat or kill. As God is my witness, I'll never be hungry again."*

I made a similar vow as I sat on my bed, sobbing. It had been one more bad day in a series of bad days—in a series of bad weeks, months, and years. I looked to my right because I always felt God was on my right, and I said, "God, I swear to you, I swear to you, one day I will have children. I will love them. I will never do to my children what my parents are doing to me."

Did I know what I was swearing? Yes. And I meant it. One doesn't make a promise to God lightly. I'd already attended years of Jewish Sunday school and Hebrew school, and I knew there was something dangerous about swearing to God. One had to be very careful when swearing to God, making a promise to him, or making an oath. I didn't exactly know why, but I knew he took the matter seriously.

I figured I'd better take it seriously as well.

*Margaret Mitchell, *Gone with the Wind* (New York: MacMillan, 1936), 161.

6

There Is No God

My father taught—or rather, drilled—the following concepts into us, because no other concepts were allowed:

"There is no god."

"There is no heaven."

"There is no hell."

"When you die, you cease to exist. There is nothing after you die. You are buried. You are forgotten."

"You are an accident of science."

"Your life has less significance than the tiniest, most microscopic speck of dust in this vast, infinite universe."

"Jesus Christ was the greatest hoax ever perpetrated on mankind."

"Paul was the biggest anti-Semite who ever lived."

"Christians are stupid for having hope."

"Christians are weak. They need a crutch. They can't see the truth."

On the other hand, he did say, "You should do the right thing because it's the right thing to do, without hope of heaven or fear of hell."

He was right about that. One should practice justice, mercy, and charity, without hope of reward or fear of punishment. Doesn't always work that way, but yes, one should behave righteously.

To some people, my father was an example of moral behavior. I didn't experience his behavior in quite the same way.

Why did he believe what he did? I don't know. It's a mystery. The rest of his family believed in God—his father, mother, brothers, and sister. They didn't live their lives in fear. My father dreaded death almost every single day of his life.

At some point, most people come to terms with their mortality. My father refused to do so.

I'm a former hospice nurse. While it's true that many people don't think much about death until they receive a terminal diagnosis, it's rare for them to pretend death doesn't exist, especially when they've outlived most of their family. My father outlived his mother, father, aunts, uncles, siblings, cousins, and even several nieces and nephews. Many of us, including my father, have at least experienced the loss of a beloved pet.

Somehow my father always assumed death wouldn't happen to him. Well, he knew in some sense it would, but he just believed that if he didn't acknowledge death, it would magically pass him by. It sounds very strange, but he blamed me for the fact of death as well.

In our family, we each had our role. Mine was that of parent to my mom, dad, and sisters, and I was the family scapegoat. My dad demanded that I wave a magic wand, play God, and make him immortal. I wanted to help him. Oh, how I tried! I tried very hard to make his wish come true, as if I could somehow control his fate.

It never occurred to me that I would live forever. Death has always been a reality for me. But as a child, I tried my best to shield my father, to assuage his fears. It never worked. I always failed because death comes, and has come, for every human being on this planet (save one who conquered death). And I was blamed for that fact.

My father's point of view was a narcissistic one. The world began and ended with him. Nothing existed before his birth, and the world would end with his death.

I'll tell you a secret. Though my father insisted there was nothing beyond death—nothing but the grave—he was lying. What he really believed was that there would be only nothingness and he'd be alone, aware of the nothingness for all eternity. That was what terrified him—an awareness of the nothingness. He would be all alone, conscious, in darkness for eternity.

Wouldn't that terrify you as well?

I realized long ago that he was right to fear. To me, this seems to be a description of exile from God. I can't imagine anything more hellish.

Regardless of my father's strident nonbelief and my mother's seeming indifference to God, I talked to God every night. I did so until I turned twelve. Then I stopped. Something happened that caused me both fear and shame. I couldn't tell anyone. I couldn't even tell God. Not only was I too ashamed to tell him, but I feared he would blame me in the same way my parents seemed to.

———

When I was twelve years old, during my preparation for study for bat mitzvah—an important coming-of-age ceremony in Judaism—my rabbi, who had been recently hired when our former rabbi moved to Florida, forced himself upon me twice a week for almost a year.

I knew deep in my bones that this was wrong. Everything he did to me was wrong.

When I fought back, tried to get away, or stop him, the rabbi slapped me, pinched me, grabbed my arm, and wrenched it behind my back. He said he loved me, that he loved me like a father, that he had my best interest at heart. But he also said if I told anyone, they wouldn't believe me—they would hate me and shun me.

Yet he claimed he did this to me only because he loved me so much, because I was so dear to him. Of course, he always added that if I didn't let him do this to me, he would hurt me.

Just like my plans to escape the Nazis, I made plans to escape this abuse. I would deliberately miss the bus after school. I was supposed to catch the downtown bus at the bus stop across the street from Hoover Elementary

54

School twice a week. Once I arrived at the downtown stop, I would walk the five or six blocks to the synagogue, where the rabbi and I would be alone for two hours. If I caught the bus right after school, I'd arrive fifteen minutes before the appointed time for my bat mitzvah study. The rabbi had insisted to my parents that I arrive fifteen minutes early so we could start class exactly on time. What it really meant was that he would have fifteen minutes to assault me.

The problem with missing the bus was that the rabbi would call my mother. She would then drive to my school, pull up to the bus stop, scream at me to get in the car, and yell at me all the way to the synagogue for being so irresponsible, for making her life so difficult. I tried to tell her that the rabbi touched me and kissed me. I didn't have the words to describe all the things he did. But every time I tried to tell her, she said, "How dare you? He's your rabbi. Don't talk about him like that. You do whatever he says."

Even my ten-year-old middle sister stood in our living room and described in graphic detail his behavior toward her and another girl her age. But my parents told her to keep quiet.

My father's mother publicly accused the rabbi of abusing his wife. He broke his wife's arm at one point, and another time he gave her a black eye. Right in front of me, my grandmother asked my parents how they could allow me to be alone with him. My mother told her to shut up.

The assaults continued. And I lived each day in anguish and shame.

Halfway through my lesson, the rabbi would take a fifteen-minute break. That meant fifteen more minutes of abuse. I was quick, so I always tried to dart past him. Often I was able to slip out of his grasp, and I ran from the classroom, calling out that I had to use the restroom. Once in the women's restroom, I hid. I kept the light off and felt my way through the room. At the far end was a narrow space between the second stall and the wall. I was skinny enough to squeeze into it.

If I didn't return to the classroom within a few minutes, the rabbi would come looking for me. He always entered the bathroom and switched on the light. I held my breath, standing as still as a stone, waiting for him to leave. He cursed and snarled, but he never found me there. Then I'd count out another ten minutes, sneak out of the bathroom, and return to the classroom.

He inevitably demanded to know where I'd been. Even in the middle of winter, I said, "I was outside." I'd get a pinch or a slap or an arm twist for my insolence. I didn't care. A bruise was better than everything else he had in mind.

I was fortunate that he was compulsive about his teaching job, and I was a dedicated student. I was his prize pupil. He never let sex stand in the way of my lesson.

———

Even after my bat mitzvah was over and the abuse had ended, even after the rabbi was caught attempting to rape a local high school girl, even after his attempted assault on our young Jewish neighbor early one morning, even after the rabbi was sent on his way to another unsuspecting congregation, I had no idea what had happened to me.

Nor did I know why it had happened. I couldn't make sense of any of it, except I knew it was wrong. I had done something very bad.

My father made it clear I was to tell no one. He went so far as to tell me not to tell him. He didn't want to know anything about the abuse, not a single detail. He said if it got out, it would reflect badly on the local Jewish community. My father was president of the congregation and had found the rabbi his next position. This was how I knew I must have done a terrible thing. I knew I was tainted.

It's ironic that in covering up the rabbi's crimes, my father hastened the demise of our Jewish community. Within a month of the rabbi's departure, there was no longer any community for my father to protect. We had no rabbi and no prospects for hiring another. Families distanced themselves from our congregation, most fleeing to synagogues in neighboring cities.

I was filled with confusion and guilt. It was my fault that our community self-destructed. At least that was how I saw it.

Through it all, my mother never said a word.

I was an innocent young girl. Neither my mother nor my father ever explained sex. I didn't understand what had happened to me until I was fourteen and my boyfriend explained it all. He said, "Old guys may think about stuff like that, but they aren't supposed to do it." He had learned about the rabbi from his brother, who was dating a girl in the clerk of courts office. She knew all about it.

My twelfth year was just one year—or perhaps I should describe it as the first year—of my struggles. The next few years were filled with turmoil; shame; confusion; sexual, physical, and emotional abuse; and an eating disorder, all culminating in a disastrous experiment with drugs and the horror of one night—a night that seemed to have been birthed directly from my father's bedtime stories.

I didn't talk to God through the years leading up to my death, though I thought about him every single day and especially at night. I missed him, but I turned my head away from him. I faced the wall. I didn't want to tell him about my failures. I didn't want him to discover the dirt that wouldn't wash off no matter how many showers I took. I couldn't allow him to know what a disgusting person I'd become.

I didn't blame God. I didn't blame anyone except myself. Part of me knew that God already knew, and that made me feel worse.

It seemed to me that I deserved whatever I got. I must have done something to deserve this kind of punishment. I believed bad people were punished. Therefore, I assumed I was a bad person.

My parents never disabused me of that notion. They were preoccupied with their own issues, and mine meant very little to them. As I mentioned previously, we children were a burden, not a joy. We were one more item on my mom's lengthy list of items she had to worry about. We weren't even on my father's list.

I'll give my mom some credit. When my weight began to drop as I ate less and less, she took me to her doctor, who for some inexplicable reason thought that my thyroid must be low. He gave me thyroid medication that sped up my metabolism, and I lost even more weight.

Here's what I've realized about anorexia, something I understood even back then. It gave me a sense of control. It was a false sense, but still, it was something. My life had spun out of control. I'd put God on the back burner. My parents provided nothing in the way of support. I had few friends, none in whom I confided. I had no anchor. The only thing I could control in my life was what I put in my mouth. So I chose to eat as little as I could.

By the time I left for Israel at the age of seventeen, I weighed eighty-two pounds. That was eighty-two pounds on a five-foot, six-inch frame. The Israelis on the kibbutz said they hadn't seen anyone look so bad since the concentration camps.

But that was still two years in the future.

My fifteenth year was my year from hell.

7

No Longer Talking to God

I'd always been at the top of my class, one of the smartest kids in school, at Kirn Junior High and Abraham Lincoln High School. Despite everything, that continued until I entered the tenth grade. When I turned fifteen, I stopped caring. I stayed near the top of my class out of pure habit, but grades no longer mattered to me.

I'd managed to survive a series of unhealthy relationships and encounters—some consensual, some not. I'd learned to lie in order to do the most ordinary things—things normal teenagers did that I wasn't allowed to do. Waterskiing or camping with friends? Canoeing and boating on Lake Manawa? Attending a chaperoned party? My parents' answer was almost always no.

As the family scapegoat, I lived in fear. I never knew which way to turn, what was coming. Whatever I did was wrong. I withdrew more and more into myself. Not only was my body shrinking, so was my soul.

At times my mother and I engaged in cathartic screaming matches. When I was backed into a corner, I lashed out at her. But I tried to avoid conflict by staying away from home as much as possible, spending time riding my horse or staying with one of my grandmothers or cousins.

Ironically, it was during this dismal period that I met the man who would later become my husband. Irwin and I met at Herzl Camp in Webster, Wisconsin. He was a regular there. I attended just one summer. I was careful to hide the truth from him and made sure he saw what I wanted him to see. I wanted him to think I was a nice person living a normal life. I kept him at arm's length—like I did almost everyone—lest he discover just how tainted I was. I assumed if he knew me, really knew me, he would reject me.

From the moment I met him, somehow I knew I would marry him, but only if I kept my life a secret. I felt unworthy of him. He was a good person. He had loving, caring parents, and they were friendly to me. I knew they liked me. I feared they would learn about the real me and hate me, shun me. I feared people would shun me, just as the rabbi had said. I had both a past and a present that were too awful to confess.

I kept my secrets, and Irwin remained my friend, at least for a time. But because of my struggles, because I pushed him away, I nearly lost him.

Before my fifteenth birthday, my boyfriend of eight months broke up with me. David, who had explained sex to me, was far from perfect, but he'd been an anchor of sorts. At least he was consistent, unlike my parents, and I'd enjoyed spending time with him. His family, especially his mother, was always welcoming and kind.

The breakup was tough. Without David and his family, I didn't have much in the way of connection. Because I'd kept my life such a secret, I also kept many people at a distance—people who otherwise would've been supportive friends. My classmates were and are wonderful people. As I've matured, we've grown closer, but back then, I was terrified they would find out the truth about my family and about me.

Several years ago, I attended my high school reunion. This was the first time I'd returned for a reunion, because even after my near-death experience, I tended to avoid things that reminded me of my life back then.

One of my classmates, Robin, a girl who had been friendly to me in high school despite my standoffishness, asked me, "Was your mom mean?"

I was taken aback. I blurted out, "What?"

She asked again, "Was your mom mean?"

"Could you be more specific?"

"I always thought your mom was mean," she said. "I remember we were at a dance team practice when she stormed in and began screaming at you. She grabbed you by your hair and dragged you out of the meeting, right in front of the entire team. We were all so scared for you, and we felt so sorry for you.

"There was another time. Do you remember that party at Lara's house? We were running around the front lawn, playing tag, having fun, just us girls, when your mom drove up. Just like before, she was screaming at you for no reason. Lara's mother ran out of the house and tried to stop her, but she threw you into the back seat of the car and drove away. We were shocked."

My eyes filled with tears. How well I remembered both of those incidents. I'd stupidly imagined I'd kept everything such a secret. I'd tried so hard to protect both my mother and me. But my friends had known and felt sorry for me. They'd seen what was happening.

I thought my heart would break. I was overwhelmed to learn that my peers had been aware of something wrong, of something bad happening to me, and they'd worried about me. They hadn't blamed me the way my parents had, the way I'd blamed myself.

I stood there feeling the shame I'd felt then. I was embarrassed for my mother, embarrassed by these public explosions. Most of the time, her explosions were a private matter. In her defense, my mother had her reasons. They may have been illogical or unfair, but in her eyes, she was justified. All the same, I couldn't deny the truth.

As you can imagine, it took me a few moments to regain my composure. "Yes," I said, my voice calm and controlled. "My mom was mean to me."

"I thought so," Robin said. "I'm sorry. I wish I could have done something."

———

Back in high school, after a few more of these sorts of humiliating episodes, I withdrew from all my longtime friends. I found myself drawn to the druggies, I suppose because they expected very little of me. I didn't have to be a good kid. I didn't have to be a bad kid. I just had to be present and uncritical to be accepted. There were no head-spinning, minute-to-minute contradictions, none of the "I never knew if I was coming or going" stuff like I experienced at home. They were all cool. Very laid-back and very stoned.

I sampled a variety of drugs, but I didn't use any drug to excess. To be honest, I didn't like anything I tried. I didn't like the way drugs made me feel. At best, I felt uncomfortable. At worst, I found the experience of getting high unpleasant. I used drugs anyway in the hope of finding some escape from my circumstances.

Several significant events occurred during this period of perhaps six to seven months. One of them was that I began dating a new guy. He was different from anyone I'd ever dated. I'll call him Tyler. He was a little older than me. He did hang with the druggies and smoked cigarettes, but he didn't drink or use drugs. He was a rangy, homely guy with long hair. He was also intelligent, honest, and trustworthy, and he radiated warmth. I found these qualities very appealing.

My father knew Tyler's mother, who'd been a classmate of his oldest brother. Nevertheless, my parents hated him. They called him ugly. They didn't like his long hair. They were upset by the fact that he smoked. They were concerned about the stability of his single-parent family. His family was poor. His mother worked full-time as a nurse to support herself and her two underage children. Tyler's older brother was already out of the house, living and working on his own. His younger sister was sweet and shy, and Tyler took care of her along with helping his mother.

Most pertinent of all, my parents despised Tyler because he was openly Christian, and worse, he'd gifted me
a dog-eared copy of the New Testament. It was a paper-
back with a blue-and-white cover. Once, I opened it to a
random page and scanned a couple verses in one of the
Gospels—Matthew, I think—but other than that, I didn't
read it. The word *hoax* kept running through my mind.
Despite that, I kept the New Testament next to my bed
because it annoyed my parents.

Tyler's religion had nothing to do with our relationship.
My previous boyfriend had been a Christian—a Catholic,
to be precise. Almost all our neighbors were Christians.
There were only a handful of us Jewish kids in my high
school—me, my younger sister and younger cousin, one
other girl my age, and one older boy. Most of the people
we knew in our small city of Council Bluffs were Christians. In fact, our small city was probably 99.9 percent
Christian.

I didn't date Tyler because he was a Christian. I dated
him because he was nice to me, he was protective of me,
and most importantly, he didn't demand sex. He intended
to save himself for marriage. This was unheard of in my
world. From my perspective, his views on sex and marriage were remarkable. The concept was brand-new to me.

In my world, virginity had never been discussed. I had
no idea whatsoever that it was something to be valued or,
for that matter, that saving oneself for marriage was even
a thing. In my world, boys and men demanded sex. Was
I supposed to resist? Whenever I did, I got hurt. I blamed
myself for the situations I found myself in, but I was un-
aware of an alternative. From the time I was twelve years

old, finding myself in abusive and dangerous situations involving sex was what passed for acceptable behavior.

This was what I'd become accustomed to. My parents never intervened. We didn't discuss boys and men and sexual abuse. In our home we had frequent discussions and arguments about Judaism, Christian anti-Semitism, the Holocaust, and politics. But self-respect, self-regard, the facts of life? I can't recall a single conversation about sexual norms and behavior between boys and girls, men and women, private or otherwise.

Naturally, I assumed everything that happened to me was all my fault. I was just a bad kid. My parents seemed to be content with that solution. I remember my mother once calling me a slut, so I was a slut. It hurt. I felt like she'd punched me in the stomach, but I shrugged and pretended I didn't care. What could I say in my own defense? Nothing.

But I knew it was a lie. I didn't dress like a slut. I deliberately dressed modestly. I rarely wore makeup. I didn't go out of my way to court male attention. I had male friends at school, one of whom is a dear friend to this day, but I didn't go looking for trouble. I knew this behavior, these situations, were wrong, yet I didn't know how to make them stop, how to make anything right.

Through all those bad times with abusive boys and men, I always told myself, *They may hurt your body, but they can't touch your soul.*

I was lying. Abuse does touch your soul.

Tyler, my boyfriend, was safe. He enjoyed my company, but he asked for nothing aside from friendship. We had fun together. We held hands. We kissed. I hung out at his house much of the time, envying his and his sister's close relationship with their mother. I've wondered on occasion if it was the powerful love I came to feel for Tyler's mother that drew me to him and his family like a magnet.

I watched in astonishment and admiration—and yes, envy—as every evening Tyler massaged his hardworking mom's aching feet. Every evening his mother brushed his sister's waist-length hair, and then she, in turn, brushed her mother's long hair. I was flabbergasted. I'd never witnessed this kind of physical affection between a parent and her children. This behavior, this sort of familial intimacy, this abundance of selflessness, was utterly foreign to me.

Tyler wasn't welcome in our home, but Tyler's mother welcomed me, making me feel like a member of the family. I was at their house almost every day after school, sitting at the kitchen table, doing homework with Tyler and his sister, staying well into the evening before walking home.

It was amazing to me that unlike the elaborate homemade meals served at my house, which were labor-intensive for my overwhelmed mother, their supper usually consisted of a can of tomato soup and a box of macaroni and cheese or grilled cheese sandwiches, a frozen pizza and a simple green salad with bottled dressing—taboo in my home—or scrambled eggs and cinnamon toast. Dessert was a carton of vanilla ice cream with four spoons, or on occasion, when Tyler's mother had a day off, tomato soup cake. I was in awe.

Tyler, his sister, and I prepared supper and set the table so all would be ready when his mother returned home from work. It wasn't the food that mattered. It was the table fellowship we shared. It was our laughter and the good-natured banter.

Their rented duplex was run-down, and it smelled of dry rot. Their furniture was old, worn, and sparse. Tyler's mother and sister shared a bedroom that had no closet. They hung their clothes on a metal rack. There were some photos on the walls but no paintings or artwork.

Tyler's family had few material possessions. What did they have? Love, and they had it in abundance.

It's true that Tyler, his mother, and his older brother smoked cigarettes. When I began to date Tyler, I started smoking, mostly to infuriate my parents. And, of course, it allowed me to eat even less.

Although I no longer talked to God, I thought about him all the time. Tyler encouraged me to begin a new conversation with him, but I refused. I had already decided I didn't want God to see me as I was. I didn't believe I deserved to talk to him. He was too good, and I was too bad.

That year, events in my life continued to spiral out of control.

8

The Muddy Trail Home

If these stories weren't crucial to my near-death experience, I would keep them hidden—for my parents' sake, not for mine. God knows all the hidden places. He knows our secrets.

When I died and returned to life, God's healing wasn't merely physical. I'd been suffering from worse injuries than just the physical. He knit my torn and broken soul back together.

During the period when I was experimenting with drugs, I had a bad day. It was Thanksgiving and many of our relatives were coming for dinner. We were expecting a houseful. My mother was extremely anxious because she had so much to do. Any event or occasion, happy or otherwise, overwhelmed her. I'd been helping her clean the house and prepare the meal, but she had been taking out her frustrations on me all day long, and I felt increasingly stressed as well.

At some point in the afternoon, I left the house, telling her I intended to visit Jason, who lived up the street. He was several years older than me and was Jewish too, and my parents were friends with his family. I'd known him my entire life. If my mother had even heard me when I told her I was leaving, she wouldn't have thought twice. She knew the family; he was Jewish. Done and done. What I didn't tell her was that Jason was a drug dealer.

When I arrived at his house, he was smoking pot with an older man I knew by sight. He was in his twenties. He, too, was a drug dealer, but he was a big-time one, part of a motorcycle gang. He'd always been polite to me, but aside from that, he'd never paid me any attention. I was just a kid, too young and insignificant to matter in his world.

This day was different. He'd brought something for Jason to try, and he offered me some as well. The two of them had been sharing a joint, but the man suggested we use his bong for his latest product.

"This is Jamaican," he said. "But I've cured it in every single drug available. I haven't tried it myself, but I have a feeling the results might be interesting."

I hadn't liked pot all that much when I'd tried it, but I was feeling adventurous. I agreed to give the bong a try, especially since this guy, who normally wouldn't give a kid like me the time of day, was offering to share. I didn't consider the consequences.

Over the next twenty minutes, the three of us shared somewhere between ten and twelve bongs of his fortified dope. I remember passing the bong to Jason, and then I knew nothing.

I regained consciousness sometime later. I had no idea if an hour had passed or if I'd been there all night. I was terrified. I had a moment of pure panic. My vision was distorted. I was hallucinating, and I had difficulty focusing on my surroundings. I could see both Jason and his friend in their chairs. Their chins were on their chests. They were unconscious. I managed to call out their names, but neither responded.

I had limited control over my movements, but I threw myself from the couch onto the floor and crawled over to them. I somehow managed to press my palm against their chests to see if they were breathing. They were still alive, but no matter how loudly I called their names or shook them, I couldn't get either of them to respond. At least I think I was calling their names. It was hard to tell what I was doing in real life and what I was doing in this awful world where reality was mixed with hallucination, overlaid by an urge to simply close my eyes and stop breathing. I had to focus on taking each breath. If I didn't concentrate, I might stop breathing and die.

And then I remembered. It was Thanksgiving. I was supposed to be home. How was I going to get there? I could barely stand up, let alone walk all the way down the hill. At the same time, I wondered if it was still Thanksgiving. I had no idea how long I'd been unconscious.

I looked outside and it was twilight, so I knew a couple hours had passed. I found a wall clock, but I couldn't make heads or tails of the time. I could no longer tell time. This alone scared me out of my wits.

What if these weird and horrible sensations and hallucinations never went away?

I somehow managed to get out the front door, down the long winding row of cement steps, and across the street. There I fell to my knees. I couldn't walk home. The ground was moving beneath me, flowing like a river.

Fortunately, I knew the trails through the woods like the back of my hand, so I let instinct take over. I crawled along the narrow, muddy, steep, winding trail, heading down the hill, and finally came to a stop when I saw the lights of my own home shining through the tree trunks. I sat for a time in a pile of leaves. Dread filled me. I didn't know what to do. I considered staying in the woods all night, but it was too cold. I wore only a pair of jeans and a thin sweater.

I forced myself to stand. Weaving, I crossed the street and quietly entered the house through the back door. All my extended family was gathered in the living room. I prayed they wouldn't see me because I was a muddy mess. I managed to get up the stairs without calling too much attention to myself. Even though I was still hallucinating, I grabbed some clean clothes and jumped into the shower. I stood there until the water was ice-cold, hoping my head would clear. It did not. Nevertheless, I got dressed and joined the festivities just as everyone was sitting down to eat.

This was bad. This was awful. Aunts, uncles, and cousins greeted me. It took so much strength and effort for me to respond appropriately to them, and to be honest, I have no idea what I said. I was too busy trying not to scream because everyone's face was distorted, appearing monstrous. I knew it was the drugs, but still, the entire experience was terrifying. My heart pounded, and I could barely catch my breath.

I couldn't eat a thing. I don't know how long I sat at the table, deaf to the conversation going on around me. Finally, I said, "I don't feel well. May I please be excused?"

My father waved me away.

I must have looked unwell, because a cousin followed me up the stairs.

"You're so pale," Carey said. "I'm worried about you."

I didn't answer. As she stood in the doorway to my bedroom, I slid under one of the twin beds and closed my eyes.

"I can't come out," I said. "I had some bad drugs. I can't see anything. I can't hear anything. I can't come out until this stuff wears off. I'm so sorry."

She sat down on the floor next to the bed and began to cry. "How can I help? Can I tell someone? Can I get someone to help you?"

"No," I said. "There's nothing you can do. Please don't tell anyone."

Carey kept my secret. She didn't tell a soul. But she did sit by the side of the bed, holding my hand, until her parents called to her that it was time to leave.

After she had gone, I crawled into bed, still in my clothes. My parents didn't come to check on me, but I didn't expect them to. I was grateful they didn't.

I didn't feel great when I awoke in the morning, but I was no longer hallucinating. The first thing I did was run up the hill to make sure Jason was still alive. He was, but he was in a heap of trouble with his father, who had come home and found Jason and his friend passed out in the living room. He'd dragged them both outside and hosed them off with cold water. Then he'd threatened them with a call to the police if Jason didn't stop using and selling drugs and if his son's business partner didn't stay away from them.

I asked Jason what was in that stuff we smoked. He said it was probably the heroin, opium, hashish, ludes, PCP, LSD, shrooms, peyote, and mescaline that just about did us all in. He said the cocaine and the meth may have kept us alive.

What did we do then? We were upset, so we proceeded to smoke a joint to calm down. Genius, right? But I'm pretty sure it was the last joint Jason smoked. Right after that, he flushed his huge hidden stash down the toilet.

I didn't quit altogether, despite Tyler's urging, but I was scared. Not scared straight, but I was really, truly frightened.

9

What Would Happen to Me Now?

Soon after that experience, I began to suffer from panic attacks. I didn't know they were panic attacks. They involved a full-blown tingling sensation in my extremities, tunnel vision, a pounding heart, and hyperventilation. It was a miracle I had never experienced a panic attack prior to this time, especially considering my life up to that point, but the experience with those drugs terrified me.

I didn't know where to go for help. I didn't know who I could talk to. One thing was for certain, I knew my parents wouldn't understand. If I told them, my life would get worse—much worse.

I kept thinking about what my cousin Carey had asked me. Could she tell someone? Could she help me? She was my age, too young to help me, but I knew a family member who might be able to—my cousin Amy, who was eight years older than me. She was engaged to be married, she'd already graduated from college, and she was experienced in the ways of the world. I admired her. She was smart and savvy and we'd always had fun together. She treated me like a valued friend, not a child.

I finally had an opportunity to speak with her. About a week later, we were all at Carey's house. I told her I wanted to call Amy to see if she would come get me. Carey grasped the situation right away. She helped me make up an excuse so our parents wouldn't worry, and I called Amy.

Amy and her fiancé were there within thirty minutes. We drove to her apartment. Amy, like all the other members of our extended family, didn't know about the abuse I'd experienced. I didn't divulge any of those secrets. I did, however, confess to her the recent experience I'd had with drugs and how it had frightened me.

Amy didn't use drugs, but she'd been to college with kids who had. She felt I should tell my parents, that they would do whatever was best for me.

I shook my head. "I don't think they'll know what to do. They'll be very upset and angry. I'm afraid to tell them."

"They love you," she said. "They don't want anything bad to happen to you. I know my parents would do whatever they had to do to help me. They would take me to the right doctor for help. If you want, I'll stay with you when you tell them."

I burst into tears. She was so smart. She possessed so much common sense, and I wanted her to be right. I desperately wanted to believe her. But she hadn't walked in my shoes. She didn't know the things I knew. She'd never seen the ugly side of my parents, the side I saw far too often. How could I tell her the truth about my life? I couldn't. I decided it was better to keep silent and continue to accept the hurt, from them and from myself. I thought, *Take your medicine like a good little girl. You deserve whatever punishment you get.*

Amy called my parents to tell them I'd be spending the night with her and that she would bring me home in the morning.

When we arrived at my house the next day, my mother was already waiting in our living room, scrunched as far back into a corner of the love seat as she could get. She was wringing her hands, and her lips were pressed tightly together. I couldn't tell if she was angry or fighting back tears, but I felt awful for causing her such distress.

My father looked grim, but he said nothing. He walked into the living room. He didn't sit beside my mother. He sat in what we called "the white chair." Amy and I followed him. I perched on the edge of the couch, Amy next to me. She patted my leg.

"Heidi has something she wants to tell you," she said and looked at me. "Go ahead, tell them."

I cleared my throat. This was so hard. I wanted to wring my hands like my mother, but I didn't. I clasped them together. "I've used drugs," I said.

My mother gasped and covered her mouth with her hand.

This wasn't something parents heard a lot back then, at least not my parents. My father still said nothing.

My voice started shaking. "I had a bad experience with drugs, and it scared me. I think I need some help."

My mother asked, "Are you a drug addict?"

"No," I said.

Amy elaborated for my sake. "Heidi isn't a drug addict. You don't have to worry about that. She hasn't used anything in a week, but as she said, she had a bad experience. There are bad drugs out there. It left her feeling very scared. That's why she called me last night. She wants some help to deal with this problem."

If I'd had the words to describe a panic attack, that was what I would've described. But I didn't. I doubt anyone did. It wasn't part of the popular lexicon back then. I assumed I was having some sort of reaction to the drugs.

My mother looked at my father. "What should we do?"

He shook his head. "It's that boyfriend."

I bristled but kept my voice even. I tried not to sound angry or defensive. "He doesn't use drugs," I said. This wasn't Tyler's fault. It was all my fault. "He's tried to stop me from using drugs."

My father didn't respond.

My mother asked, "Should I talk to Dr. Carson?"

As I mentioned before, Dr. Carson was our neighbor. He was a general practitioner who had completed medical school but had not done a residency. He was my grandmother's physician. My pediatrician had died suddenly when I was twelve years old, and my parents had never taken me to another one. If I was sick or injured, they always called Dr. Carson. He would walk across the street, give them his opinion, and walk back home.

I missed my pediatrician. He'd saved my life when I was seven years old and had developed an intussusception—a serious condition that causes an intestinal blockage—in the middle of the night. As I sat there thinking about Dr. Carson and about how little interest he had in me and in my welfare, I wished my pediatrician was still alive.

Then I thought, *It doesn't matter. You are a bad person, a bad daughter. You've frightened your mother half to death, and your father is furious and disappointed. You've let them down again. Dr. Carson's disinterest is exactly what you deserve.*

We all sat in silence. My mother finally broke it. "I'll talk to Dr. Carson," she said. "He'll know what we should do."

I doubted that. Dr. Carson was a strict Catholic, and as my father frequently emphasized to us, his children were perfect. I knew for a fact his children would never screw up the way I had. But this decision wasn't up to me, and at that moment, I was willing to do whatever I had to do to get rid of the horrible episodes of panic, even if it meant asking for help from someone in whom I had little confidence.

I hugged my cousin, thanking her for her support, and she got up to leave. My parents accompanied her to the door and thanked her for bringing me home. They left me sitting alone in the living room, staring down at the floor. There were no hugs. There were no words of comfort or encouragement. No one said to me, "It will be okay. We love you, and we'll find a way to help you."

I spent the day alone in my room.

That evening, Dr. Carson dropped by. He spoke with my parents, and they called me into the living room.

"I've given your parents the name of a psychiatrist," he said. "He'll see you this week."

My parents both looked at me. I nodded my agreement. Of course I would see him. I was desperate to get rid of what had become an ever-present anxiety. Ironically, the sensation of panic was dissipating, but now, especially around my parents, I felt this awful anxiety in the pit of my stomach. I knew they hated me for what I'd done. It was like with the rabbi all over again. I'd done something awful, and it seemed they believed I'd done it deliberately to hurt them, to cause them difficulties and embarrassment.

I hadn't intended to hurt them. I'd experimented with drugs to try to mask my own pain. But I agreed with my parents' assessment. I was a bad person, and I did bad things. That was the message I had internalized. I was a major screwup.

For the next few days, I tiptoed around the house. I spoke when spoken to, but otherwise I kept silent and stayed out of everyone's way. In any case, my parents barely acknowledged me. They occasionally cast furtive glances in my direction, looking at me as if I were a leper and contact was to be avoided at all costs. My sisters were encouraged to keep their distance. I had really messed up this time.

Not only did my parents give me the silent treatment, but I punished myself every second of every day. And I lived in a constant state of fear. What would happen to me now?

10

Meeting Dr. Kitts

The only way I can describe Dr. Kitts, the man who would be my psychiatrist, is to say there was nothing warm and fuzzy about him. He didn't smile or shake my hand. He didn't say, "It's nice to meet you. I look forward to working with you. Have a seat." He didn't ask, "How can I help you?" He didn't say, "I'm sure I can help you with this problem."

In other words, he didn't exactly inspire confidence, nor was he welcoming. He wasn't flat-out cold, but I can't even describe his manner as matter-of-fact or professional. He simply seemed disinterested.

I felt uneasy in his office. I sat on the edge of my chair, ready to bolt at any moment.

Dr. Kitts didn't ask me many questions aside from my age and my grade in school, and he seemed to already know what my answers would be. His initial questions felt like a mere formality. I didn't volunteer much information. He didn't take the lead, and I wasn't certain what to say.

What did one tell a psychiatrist on the first visit? How much did he already know? I wasn't sure I could trust him, so I was guarded. A psychiatrist was supposed to keep everything confidential, but I had a nagging suspicion he'd made an agreement with my parents to tell them what was said in these sessions.

At last, he asked, "Do you know why you're here?"

"Yes," I said. "I used some bad drugs, and the experience scared me a lot. I asked for help. My parents talked to our neighbor, and he gave them your name."

"Do you still use drugs?"

"I've smoked a little pot, but I haven't used anything else since that time."

"I understand you smoke."

"Do you mean cigarettes?"

"Yes, cigarettes. Why do you smoke?"

Yes, he had clearly spoken with my parents.

I shrugged. "All my friends smoke."

"You have a boyfriend?"

"Yes."

"And does he use drugs as well?"

"No, he doesn't use drugs."

"Are you sure?"

"Yes, I'm sure. He doesn't use drugs."

"What about your other friends? Do they use drugs?"

"Yes, most of them."

"The same drugs you use?"

I shook my head. "No. They use harder drugs than I use."

"I see. Do you have sex with your boyfriend?"

That question surprised me. "No."

"Have you ever had sex with your boyfriend?"

"No. He doesn't believe in premarital sex."

"Do you?"

This came out of left field. I began to stutter and stammer. "I don't know . . ."

"Why not?"

I just shrugged. I wanted to say, *Because no one ever told me about sex before I had sex, before the rabbi assaulted me, so I don't really have an opinion.* But I stayed silent.

He fiddled with his pen. "I have six children," he said.

"Oh." I wasn't quite sure what that bit of information had to do with anything.

"My oldest just turned fourteen. My youngest is two."

"Uh-huh. That's nice." Maybe he was worried about them. I wondered if I should ask him a question about his life. Wasn't he supposed to be asking the questions?

Since he said nothing else, I assumed he expected a response from me. "Are you concerned they will use drugs?"

"No. The older children attend Catholic school."

"Okay. That's good." Was I doing this psychiatrist thing wrong?

We spoke briefly about their Catholic school and then sat in silence. I watched as he appeared to jot down a few notes.

After another few minutes, he looked up from what I assumed was my chart. "I'll see you next week, then."

"Um, okay?" Yeah, I had to be doing this psychiatrist thing wrong.

The next session followed the same pattern, although there were no more questions about drugs. He asked me a few questions about school and my friends. He asked me if I was still smoking cigarettes and if I had the same boyfriend. Then we talked about his family. I heard about his wife, her terrible headaches, her awful gelatin-and-carrot salad, how his oldest daughter played tennis, how his oldest son liked to golf at their country club. I learned that Dr. Kitts hated tomatoes. He didn't much like lettuce either, unless it came smothered in blue cheese dressing. He was a steak-and-potatoes kind of guy.

By our third session, I was angry and frustrated. It seemed as if we were getting nowhere. When I sat down, once again he began our conversation by telling me what his children had been doing all week. I heard about plans for Christmas break and about how his wife was toilet training his youngest child.

"This feels pointless," I said. "Aren't you supposed to be asking me questions?"

He looked up from his scribbling. "Questions about what?"

"I don't know. You're the psychiatrist. Aren't you supposed to ask me questions about my family? Dreams? Freud asked his patients about their dreams."

"Do you want me to ask you about your dreams?"

"I want you to ask me about something that matters. I want you to ask about what happened to me the night I used those drugs and got really scared. Ask me why I use drugs. Maybe you can help me figure out why I use drugs.

Ask questions about how I'm feeling. You have never once asked me how I'm feeling."

"How you're feeling about what?"

I probably could have been more respectful, but I rolled my eyes. "Like, if I still have those times when I get scared, when my heart pounds and I feel like I'm going to faint. Questions about that. That's why I wanted to get help in the first place."

He tapped his pen. It seemed like he loved that pen. "Well, how are you feeling?"

"I'm upset. There are still times when it happens. It scares me."

"Why does it scare you?"

"Because I feel like I'm going to die. When it happens, I feel like I'm going to pass out and die."

I have no idea if he recognized these symptoms as what are now called panic attacks or panic disorder. He gave no indication that he did. I do know that even back then, hyperventilation was recognized by the medical establishment, hence the television trope about breathing into a paper bag. But I didn't know about hyperventilation or panic attacks. I just knew that when I was under stress, my heart would pound, my respiration would increase, I would feel tingling in my arms and legs, and I'd experience tunnel vision. When this occurred, I was terrified. And I didn't know what to do when I was in the middle of one of these attacks.

"I've never observed an episode," Dr. Kitts said. "You haven't had one here in this office."

"I can't make it happen by snapping my fingers," I replied. "I have no control over this. It might happen at school or when I'm at home with my family. I never know. That's what makes it so scary."

"So, are you saying you feel safe in my office?"

I thought about that. "I don't know. It hasn't happened here, but I'm only here for maybe thirty minutes. I suppose it could happen here, eventually. It even happens when I'm with my boyfriend, and I feel safe with him."

Dr. Kitts began tapping his pen again. "How would you feel about inpatient therapy?"

"You mean be admitted to a mental hospital? No, I don't want that."

"Oh, it's not like that," he said. "This is voluntary, and it's an open ward. It's very modern, like a dormitory. None of the doors are locked. You can leave anytime you like. You could participate in group therapy and see me once a day. Right now, there are a few other kids your age. And there would be trained staff around to help you if you feel afraid."

I sat in silence, considering this option. "What about my parents? I don't think they would like it. I think this would embarrass them. I already embarrass them."

I'd just given him another opening, but he didn't comment on my statement. He didn't ask why I thought I embarrassed my parents.

"I can talk to your parents," he said.

"Can I have visitors?"

"Yes, of course, with some limitations."

"What limitations? What about my boyfriend? Can he visit? Or other friends? Or just my parents?"

"Well, your parents will be able to visit. If your boyfriend or your other friends want to visit, I have no objection.

But the visits will have to be in the common room, and there is no drug use allowed."

"Yes, of course. No drugs."

He continued tapping his pen. "What do you think?"

"It would be sort of a place where I could get better, right? A place where I wouldn't feel any stress or pressure?"

"I suppose you can look at it that way."

"I want to feel better."

"Let me talk to your parents. If they agree, I can admit you tomorrow."

I nodded. I was willing. I wanted to feel better. I was desperate to feel better.

I imagined this experience would be like going to camp. The more I thought about it, the more I felt that getting away from my parents and the stress I faced at home was a step in the right direction. I was a little nervous about going to a psychiatric hospital, but Dr. Kitts had said it was an open ward, not something straight out of Ken Kesey's *One Flew Over the Cuckoo's Nest*. And I could leave whenever I wanted to. I would check myself in, and if I didn't like it, I would check myself out.

From my perspective, I had nothing to lose and a whole lot to gain.

11

The Ward

It was December, a little over four months before my accident, and it was almost Christmas break. The day after talking with Dr. Kitts, I packed my bag. I didn't need much—toiletries, a hairbrush, underwear, pajamas, socks, a couple pairs of jeans and my favorite corduroys, a few sweaters and T-shirts, a pair of sneakers. That was it, all I needed.

My mother drove me to the facility. It wasn't far from our house—a little over a mile. She checked me in at the main desk and drove away. A nurse dressed in street clothes escorted me to the unit.

Dr. Kitts had described the facility accurately. It was brand-new. Everything was clean and bright. There were loads of windows. Each person had a private room and bathroom. The nurses' station was just a desk, and the nurses dressed in street clothes, like the patients. For the most part, the nurses were young, and I was told to call them by their first names. A couple of the charge nurses were older, perhaps in their forties.

I was given a tour. Our first stop was my room. My bag was opened and searched, and the nurse watched while I put my things away. The razor I'd brought to shave my legs was confiscated. That didn't upset me. I should have realized a razor wouldn't be allowed. I saw the dining room, the game room, the room for arts and crafts, and the room for group therapy. In front of the nurses' desk was a lounge area with couches and chairs and a large television.

There was a telephone at the nurses' station and another in the lounge. I was told we were allowed to make brief phone calls if we first received permission from the doctor or the staff and that the staff would listen in. Dr. Kitts's office was located behind the nurses' station.

We weren't allowed to leave the facility without filling out some paperwork. We could go to a scheduled medical appointment or on an outing with family members, but since this was an inpatient unit, proper procedures had to be followed. The staff and my psychiatrist had to be notified in advance if I was leaving the ward.

My stomach did more than a few flip-flops. I'd always been shy, and I was a little overwhelmed, wondering what I'd gotten myself into. I felt claustrophobic too, but the ward did seem to be a nice place. The staff was friendly and helpful. I hoped for the best, but I was unsure of myself, and I was unsure whether this inpatient stay would provide the help I needed.

The other patients were pleasant enough. There were perhaps twelve of them. Most were adults, but there was one boy I knew from school, Andy. I greeted him, both surprised and relieved to see a familiar face. There was also a girl a little younger than me. She didn't speak to me at all that first day.

I wasn't expected to participate in anything until the next day. This first day was my orientation to the ward and the schedule of activities.

I had lunch and supper that day. I watched a little television with the rest of the patients, and then I went to bed, leaving the door to my room halfway open as instructed. I slept fitfully, both because the light was kept on in the hallway, which made my room too bright to sleep soundly, and because a nurse peeked in on me several times.

At breakfast I sat with Andy. The girl who hadn't spoken to me the day before sat with us. Andy introduced us. Her name was Joy.

"Here she comes," Joy said without looking up from her oatmeal.

"Who?" I asked.

"The med nurse."

"Med nurse?"

"Use your tongue," Joy said. "Spit them back into your milk carton."

"What?"

The nurse stopped at our table and handed Joy a little paper cup. "Here you go," she said.

Joy tipped the cup into her mouth, then she took a few swallows of her chocolate milk from the carton.

"Open."

Joy opened her mouth to show the nurse that she had swallowed the pills.

The nurse turned to me. "Your doctor has ordered these," she said. She showed me a similar little cup containing three pills.

"What are these?" I asked.

"These are the medications your doctor has ordered. They will help you."

"But he didn't tell me about any medication. I don't want to take anything until I have a chance to talk to him."

"He'll speak with you after breakfast, after you take your pills."

This wasn't something I had anticipated. "I don't want to take any pills. He didn't say anything about pills."

"Sorry, you must take these. Rules are rules. He ordered them. You take them."

I didn't have a milk carton, and even if I had, I didn't know how to spit the pills into the carton in a way that wouldn't be obvious. I took the three pills.

Within forty minutes, I could barely move my mouth to form a coherent word. The floors rolled beneath my feet, and my head was spinning off into space. I felt doped up. My body was heavy. My feet felt like lead. This was almost as bad as the night I had used those drugs. What on earth had she given me?

I had to be guided to Dr. Kitts's office and helped into a chair. I could see him—sort of—when I managed to focus my eyes. I clearly remember mumbling, "I don't want to take those pills."

I clearly remember his answer. "Those pills will make you better."

And I clearly remember mine. "I don't feel better. I feel worse."

Neither of us said another word. He made some notes on my chart, and the nurse escorted me to my room. I collapsed onto the bed and slept for the rest of the day. I couldn't be roused for anything—not group therapy, not arts and crafts, not a game of pool. I was out.

At suppertime, the nurse came in to wake me. I stumbled to the dining room but was unable to eat anything. I managed to find my way back to my room, undress myself, and get into bed. Sometime later, I woke with a start, confused, unsure of where I was. Then I remembered. The psychiatric hospital. The pills. My head ached and I felt rotten, like I imagined someone with a hangover would feel.

I lay there in the half-light, thinking, *No more pills*. No way. I would spit them into a milk carton even if I choked to death. And if they forced me to take those pills, I would go home. I would check myself out.

The next day, I learned I couldn't check myself out.

Dr. Kitts had lied to me, as had my parents. I could leave only with their permission. Not only did I feel sick as a dog physically, I felt heartsick.

I'd been betrayed.

I grabbed a carton of chocolate milk and received a crash course from Joy on how to spit out my pills. She also taught me how to behave as though I'd taken them. Be quiet. Look drowsy. Follow instructions. Less is more.

She helped me regain a small sense of control, but mostly I just felt hollow, lost, angry. I'd been honest with my parents. I'd gone to them, albeit reluctantly, seeking their help, seeking the comfort and protection a parent should provide a child.

Instead, they'd done it again. Provided no comfort or protection, betrayed my trust, and ripped away what little control I had over my own life. They had lied to me. I wasn't surprised. What had I expected? At this point in time, our communication was nonexistent, our relationship beyond strained.

I will admit that during my stay in the psychiatric hospital, I no longer suffered from panic attacks. But within ten days, I had a lot more to worry about than irrational fear. Within ten days, I knew what real fear felt like.

12

"They Don't Love Me"

I was greatly relieved I was no longer having panic attacks, but I had no idea if I felt better because I was away from my family and out of my usual dysfunctional routine, or if the fear had simply worn off because I wasn't using drugs. Dr. Kitts and I had never discussed it. I found that odd. But then, he and I didn't talk about much. Sometimes he asked me about my interests or my favorite classes at school. Perhaps he was aware of what had happened with the rabbi, perhaps not. He never gave any indication he knew. Our daily sessions lasted no more than three minutes.

I once asked him why we spent so little time together. He said, "It's because I get information from the staff about your progress."

I was friendly with many of the people in the unit, but I rarely spoke during group therapy, and even when I did, it was usually to sympathize with another patient. I had yet to divulge much of anything about my own situation, aside from admitting I had used drugs and had had a frightening experience with them. I didn't know how to talk about my parents. For one thing, they were my parents. For another, they had a sterling reputation in the community. I didn't want to tarnish it.

My circumstances weren't typical, nor were Dr. Kitts's methods. I was still spitting out my pills and I wasn't depressed. I hadn't attempted suicide, nor did I have suicidal thoughts, as did many of my fellow patients, including Andy from my high school. I wasn't imagining little green men or monsters. I didn't spout nonsense or have conversations with invisible people.

Yes, I had defied my parents. I had broken their rules, and my mother and I had been fighting. Yes, I'd experimented with drugs. Yes, they didn't like my boyfriend. But those circumstances didn't warrant me being in this place.

Oddly enough, my parents had never complained about my previous boyfriend, the one with whom I'd had a sexual relationship. Perhaps because he was clean-cut? Because he didn't smoke cigarettes? Or because he hadn't given me a copy of the New Testament?

My parents and I had a big to-do via proxy. I'd been in the inpatient unit for about ten days. I was cooperative and pleasant. I participated in group therapy, although that mostly involved listening to the adults talk about their relationships. Sadly, many of them were depressed and had either threatened or attempted suicide. Fortunately, they or a family member had recognized they were depressed and sought help, not just from Dr. Kitts but from another psychiatrist in attendance.

I spent time in the art room, painting and working with clay. I played pool and poker and gin rummy. Sometimes the games involved just us three teens, but quite often the adults would play with us. Most of the adult patients had children of their own. They were lonely, and they sort of adopted us. Together we became like a surrogate family.

Despite my parents' complaints, I continued to smoke cigarettes. At this point, I did so for two reasons, neither of which had anything to do with my parents. First, smoking was a companionable activity. Most of the other patients smoked.

Second, I could get outdoors. Even though it was December, it was a pleasure and a relief to get some fresh air. We were allowed outside only to smoke; otherwise we would be stuck indoors. A nurse accompanied us and held the cigarette lighter, and we were each allowed one cigarette three times per day. I didn't mind. We laughed and joked while we were out in the courtyard. I had spent much of my life outdoors in all kinds of weather, and I missed that freedom terribly.

Overall, I really did try to get along. I was agreeable. I was cheerful. I knew the other patients and the nurses liked me. I caused no trouble for anyone.

Then one day, about ten days into my stay, Dr. Kitts informed me I was no longer allowed to smoke. He added,

"No more phone calls to your boyfriend and no more visits from him. From now on, you're only allowed calls and visits from your parents."

My boyfriend had visited on a single occasion. I'd followed the rules and made sure to get permission in advance from Dr. Kitts and the staff. Tyler and I sat together on the couch in front of the nurses' desk, holding hands and watching television. He'd been allowed to stay for one hour, and Dr. Kitts had specified the hour.

My only other visitor had been my mother. She'd visited twice, once to bring me an article of clothing I needed, and the second time to visit me for about fifteen minutes. She was allowed into my room. We didn't have much to say to each other, but our time together wasn't unpleasant. I showed her some of my projects in the art room. My father had not come with her, nor had he come to see me on his own.

I hadn't asked permission for visits with anyone besides Tyler, and I was shocked by the new rules. I sat in Dr. Kitts's office, staring at him. I simply couldn't comprehend why he would refuse my boyfriend permission to visit. "Why? What did I do wrong?"

He shrugged. "Your parents think it's in your best interest if you don't see him, and they don't want you smoking."

"But . . ." I didn't know what to say. I felt powerless. I blurted out, "I didn't do anything wrong, but I'm being punished. That's not fair."

"What's not fair?"

"They get to decide everything in my life, out there and in here. It's not fair."

"They're your parents. They know what's best for you."

"But you've already given Tyler permission to come this afternoon."

"He'll be sent home. I've left orders at the desk downstairs."

He dismissed me. I left his office, crying, and ran to my room. One of the nurses, the one I liked the best, followed me.

I threw myself across my bed and sobbed. She sat down next to me and put her hand on my back. "It's okay," she said. "You're doing well. Hopefully you'll be out of here in a few weeks and you can get back to your normal life."

"I don't have a normal life," I cried. "And it's not mine, it's theirs. It's always been theirs. My parents don't care about me. They're punishing me, even in here."

She tried to comfort me. "Your parents care about you. They love you."

I sat up and faced her. "You're wrong. They don't love me. They don't even know me. Tyler is the only good thing I have in my life. He's the only person who cares about me, and now I can't see him."

"Look, I know you're upset and angry, but things will look different in the morning. Things will get better."

"When?" I threw myself back across the bed. She took the hint and left me alone. I didn't think things were ever going to get better.

I had no appetite that evening, so I skipped supper. I was angry with my parents, angry with Dr. Kitts, angry with the staff for enforcing his stupid rules. I was angry

I'd been lied to, betrayed. I was angry that I could leave only with my parents' permission, angry that I had to spit pills into a milk carton.

I was just plain angry. I sulked in my room. Again, the nurse I liked the best came in. She tried to reason with me, telling me things would look better in the morning, that I was being overly dramatic—which I was.

In the middle of our conversation, she was called away. I took the opportunity to walk out the emergency exit door, right into the cold, snowy December night.

Of course, the alarms went off, and I broke into a run. Before I knew it, I'd run the six blocks to Tyler's house. It wasn't my intention to run away and disappear. I simply wanted to see him, to explain to him that the no-contact rule wasn't my idea. In truth, I escaped because I wanted to hurt my parents.

Tyler's mother answered the door. She was horrified to see me standing there in jeans and a T-shirt, soaked to the skin. She grabbed me by the shoulders and pulled me into her house, slamming the door behind me. She sent me upstairs to take a warm bath. While my clothes dried in the dryer, she wrapped me in her bathrobe and sat me down at the kitchen table. She handed me a cup of hot chocolate and stood beside me, placing a hand on my shoulder in a reassuring way. She was a kind, caring woman, a good mother.

"I'm going to call your parents," she said.

I begged her not to.

She stroked my hair. "Honey, it's the right thing to do. They must be frantic."

I could see the worry in her eyes, so I made no further protest. At that moment, Tyler and his younger sister walked in. He saw me and burst into tears. He'd been worried about me, especially after he'd come to visit and been turned away.

Regret washed over me. I was sorry to have upset them. I wished I hadn't come. I wanted a do-over. I wanted to just turn around and walk myself back to the hospital, because I knew there would be a scene. Tyler's mother urged me to wait for my parents. I couldn't stop apologizing because I knew this would get ugly and it was all my fault.

My parents arrived thirty minutes later. Tyler's mother sent me upstairs with my now dry clothes. As I dressed, I heard her downstairs, trying to reason with my parents. Her voice was soft, controlled, and calm. She was attempting to have a rational conversation.

I sat at the top of the stairs beside Tyler's sister, hugging my knees. I heard Tyler's mother say, "Heidi is welcome to stay here for the night. She'll be safe here. She agreed to stay. I'll make sure she does. She can sleep in my bed with me. We can all talk this over in the morning, when everyone is calm."

My parents' response was cold and cruel, to her and to Tyler. They told her in no uncertain terms to mind her own business.

I was grateful to her, but I felt terribly guilty. She was trying to help me, but she was getting nowhere, and I had put her in this untenable position. Tyler was crying and was confrontational, both of which hardened my parents' hearts.

I'd made a terrible mistake. I had involved Tyler and his mother and even his sister in a private family matter. This was bad.

I got to my feet and descended the stairs, knowing there would be consequences. I figured they would be significant. But I wasn't prepared for what lay ahead.

13

"Mom, Please Don't Do This"

I could have run again, but I didn't. Tyler's mother had attempted to intervene on my behalf. I had put her in a difficult position, and I felt running away would add insult to injury and would betray her trust in me. I didn't want to cause her any more pain or distress. She worked hard enough to support her own family. She didn't need to be my emotional support as well. Worse, I'd heard my father threaten her with legal action for harboring a runaway: me. I was horrified.

For good or for ill, I wasn't concerned about causing my own mother and father pain and distress. I didn't think they would care if I ran away again. I was convinced they would be happier not to deal with me at all. I believed that in their hearts, they'd be relieved if I just disappeared. Certainly, their lives would be easier. They'd told me that repeatedly; to use their words, I was a burden to them and I would amount to nothing.

Regardless, it was time to face the music. I hugged Tyler's mother. We both had tears streaming down our cheeks. I followed my parents to the car and climbed into the back seat.

I knew my parents were returning me to the inpatient facility. Although the drive was short, I made those two minutes as miserable for them as I could, telling them what bad parents they were and how much I hated them.

My behavior was inexcusable. I'm not proud of myself. I wanted to hurt them as much as they'd hurt me. I don't know if I succeeded. This kind of confrontation was out of character for me. I'd never taken pleasure in hurting others. My first option had always been to blame myself.

Everything I said to them, every word out of my mouth, came from years of internalized pain. It all came out— the pain, the hurt, the neglect, the abuse I'd experienced. Did I hate them, as I claimed? Not really. Did I wish I had different parents? Absolutely. Did I mean to hurt them? Only in that moment.

My parents were silent as we rode in the car. I didn't blame them at the time, and I don't blame them now. I assumed even then that Dr. Kitts had instructed them not to respond to anything I said.

When we turned the wrong way—when my father didn't drive to the entrance of the modern inpatient unit—I fell silent. My stomach twisted into a knot, and I wondered what sort of punishment my parents and Dr. Kitts had cooked up for me.

My father pulled up to an old building, an ancient building. Everyone in town knew about this place. It was the Catholic psychiatric hospital, known for warehousing the chronically ill.

A wave of fear washed over me. I had known there would be a price to pay for my actions. I just didn't know how steep it would be.

"Why are we here?" I asked. "I thought we were going back to the new section."

My mother said, "We are, but the desk is closed, and the doctor told us to check you in here."

I didn't believe her.

She and I got out of the car. My father stayed behind the wheel, staring straight ahead.

He hadn't said a single word to me since he'd walked into Tyler's house. I looked over my shoulder as I got out of the car, studying his face. I could see only his profile.

"Dad? What's going on?"

He didn't answer. He continued to stare straight ahead.

I followed my mother into the building. The main door opened into nothing but a dark, narrow hallway. At the far end were two elevators. She walked straight to the elevators and pressed the button.

"Mom? What's going on? Mom? What are you doing?"

The elevator door opened, and there stood two beefy orderlies. I let out a strangled cry. Ice-cold terror filled my veins.

In desperation, I turned to my mother. I held out my arms to her. "No, Mom, no, don't do this. Please don't do this. I'm sorry. Mom, please don't do this. I'm sorry."

She stepped back, and as the orderlies dragged me into the elevator, I watched her turn toward the exit and walk away.

The men pressed against me, one on my right, the other on my left. Each had a firm grip on one of my arms.

My entire body froze with fear. I whispered, "Where are we going?"

It was a rhetorical question. I already knew the answer.

They were silent. Then one man reached over and pushed the button for the fourth floor. That was the horrible floor. I'd heard rumors.

"No," I said, my voice rising. "No. You can't . . . You can't make me. I'm not going there. No."

But up we went to the fourth floor.

The elevator opened onto an empty corridor. At the far end was a locked metal gate.

I was screaming now, pleading with them. "No, I'm not going! No, please don't take me there. Please, don't take me there! Please let me go!"

They ignored my pleas, so I fought tooth and nail, kicking, screaming, struggling to get out of their tight grip.

As the man on my right reached for a ring of keys, I slipped from his grasp and dropped to the floor. My fingernails scraped along the linoleum tiles as I tried in vain to crawl away while the other man dragged me toward the gate.

He tackled me before I could get to my feet and run, just as the first man finished unlocking the gate. The first man turned back to grab one of my ankles and tried to pull me through the opening, but I wrapped my arms around the metal bars and held on with all my strength, screaming for help at the top of my lungs.

I heard other screams, moans, groans, and cries, and I knew I was being dragged through the gates of hell.

One of the men pried my arms, hands, and fingers from the bars as the other tried to get a grip on my ankles. He couldn't keep hold of both ankles because I kept kicking at him with my free leg. The men managed to drag me through the gate. They tossed me against a wall.

I lay there, stunned, the breath knocked out of me. That was when I saw them—the inmates. Old, bedraggled, filthy, barefoot. All of them staring at me, eyes wide, echoing my screams of terror.

I tried to sit up, to crawl away, but the men grabbed me again, flinging my body up in the air. One man pinned my legs against his chest, and the other wrapped his arms around my torso, pinning my arms to my sides.

I fought them, trying to break free, screaming for help as they carried me past the horde of zombie-like creatures into a small, padded cell. In the room stood a woman dressed in a white nurse's uniform, complete with a little nurse's hat.

"Help me," I cried. "Please help me."

She said nothing. She motioned to the orderlies, and they began tugging at my clothing. I fought them bitterly. I knew I was no match for them, but I fought them with the desperation of a cornered animal.

In the end I stood there naked.

The nurse made another motion. One of the orderlies reached for my glasses.

That was the moment I broke.

My soul shattered. I fell to my knees and pressed my hands together in supplication, begging, pleading.

"No," I said, sobbing. "No, not my glasses. I'm helpless without them. Please, don't take my glasses. Please, don't take my glasses."

It was true. I was so severely nearsighted that I was helpless without my glasses.

The men held my arms, and the nurse took my glasses, folded them, and stuck them in her breast pocket.

The men lifted me off the floor and stretched me out on a bed. I tried to resist, but doing so was futile. One man lay over my body while the other tied my right wrist into a restraint, then my left wrist. Then they each took a leg and tied a restraint around each ankle.

The nurse walked toward me and removed something from the pocket of her uniform. It was a hypodermic needle.

"No. No. Please don't do this. Please don't do this. I'm begging you, please. I'll do anything, anything you ask."

But she stuck that needle into my thigh, injecting who knows what, and she did it without any expression on her face and without a word.

The three of them turned and left, shutting the padded door, shutting out all light but that which came from a tiny slit window near the top of the door.

Tears streamed down the sides of my face. My body shook with shock and cold. My teeth chattered. It was freezing in there on that bare mattress. I was absolutely, utterly helpless.

The Nazis had come, and I'd been caught unawares. It was Richard. Speck. And I'd had no way to defend myself.

My father was right. There was no such thing as hope. His nightmare bedtime stories were all true; each word he'd said was true.

I knew with every fiber of my being that if left here in this padded cell, I would die. Worse, if I was let out into that ward of horrors, I would lose my mind. I hadn't lost my mind, but it was crystal clear to me that if Dr. Kitts and my parents left me in this situation long enough, I would.

Death was the better option.

I wanted to die. I wanted to die more than anything. I turned to God. At long last, I turned to God, and I prayed for death.

I prayed for death with all my heart.

I prayed for death with all my soul.

I prayed for death with all my strength.

If my father was right that there was no hope, then an eternity of nothingness would be a million times better than this. It would be infinitely better.

In that moment of utter despair, a light fell across my face. Despite my extreme nearsightedness, I followed its trajectory. The light came through the blackened caged window to my right. Near the top of the window, it seemed as if someone had scraped off a circle of the dark film or black paint covering the reinforced glass. How someone managed to get eight feet off the ground and reach through the bars to do that, I didn't know and I didn't care, because there in the center of the circle was the full moon. At least

I thought it was the moon. What else could it be? I was so nearsighted I couldn't tell. I assumed the sky had cleared since I'd been dragged into this hellish place.

I focused all my attention on the light and on the God who'd provided this light in my darkness. If it was the moon, it seemed as if it had slowed its normal progress. I could see it for hours, for the entire night, although I knew that was impossible.

My tears dried. I ignored the cold. I kept my eyes glued to that light all night long, thanking God repeatedly for this one blessing.

And that is how I survived the night.

14

A Tiny Glimpse of Heaven

The next morning, I heard a key turn in the lock.

The door opened. I turned my head from the window. A different nurse entered the room, a young woman.

I said nothing. I merely looked at her. I was too weak to utter a single word.

She undid the restraints, massaged my numb hands and feet, arms and legs, and helped me stand. I swayed on my feet, so she hurriedly sat me on the side of the bed. Dressing was next to impossible; my arms, legs, hands, and feet were too stiff and cold.

The nurse dressed me. She knelt to slip on my socks and shoes and tied the laces. She pulled my glasses out of a pocket and placed them back on my nose.

If I'd been able to speak (speech was beyond me at that point), I would have thanked her, but I think she understood when she saw the tears streaming down my face.

I could read her expression. She was upset at finding me in this condition. She seemed kind. Perhaps she would help me, protect me from a fate worse than death.

I was afraid to hope, and I was almost too numb to care.

She held me tight as she escorted me to the enclosed, locked nurses' station. I couldn't go inside, but she pulled a clean chair from within and placed it right next to the plexiglass door.

"Sit," she said. "And don't move. I'll keep an eye on you."

I practically fell into the chair. As the curious residents milled about me, poking and prodding, tugging at my long hair, I pulled my knees up to my chest and rested my head on my hands. I closed my eyes. I didn't have the strength to push them away, and I couldn't look at them. I feared I would become like them.

The nurse unlocked the door. She shooed all the residents away and handed me a cup of orange juice. "Drink this."

I drank it. Something inside told me I could trust her not to medicate me against my will. It was just a plastic cup of prepackaged orange juice, but nothing had ever tasted better.

She repeated her instructions: "Sit here and don't move. They won't hurt you. I'm trying to get you back to the other ward as quickly as possible. I hope someone will come to escort you back before breakfast."

I could only communicate with my eyes. I was too bruised and exhausted, physically and emotionally, to do otherwise. But I could tell she understood, because she nodded and gave me what I interpreted as a reassuring smile.

I sat there for perhaps another thirty minutes, trying to make myself as small a target as possible. At last, the gate was unlocked. It clanked open and closed, and one of the nurses from my unit walked in. She passed right by me, placing a hand on my shoulder for just a moment before she entered the med room and shut the door behind her. The two nurses put their heads together and seemed to speak urgently. I couldn't hear them, but it was clear both were upset.

After several minutes, the nurse from my unit exited the plexiglass booth. She took my arm. "You can come with me."

I looked into her eyes, studied her face. I cleared my throat and tried to speak. My throat was very sore, and I could barely manage a hoarse whisper. "Where are we going?"

"To the other unit," she said.

We remained silent as we made our way through the milling horde. Some of the residents reached out, trying to touch me, but the presence of the nurse kept them at bay. They still frightened me, but at the same time I pitied them. They had to stay in this terrible place, locked in their own personal hells, for the rest of their lives.

Meanwhile, the nurse and I went through the gate. She locked it behind her. It wasn't until we stood in the elevator and the door closed that I asked, "Why?"

She shook her head. "There are some people waiting for you."

"Who?" My stomach churned. *Please tell me it's not my parents. Please tell me it's not my parents.*

"You don't realize how many friends you have," she said. And then she gave me a little smile.

Her words made no sense to me.

I followed her into the open ward. She stepped aside, and I was immediately surrounded by all the other patients. They hugged me, kissed me, mussed my already tangled hair, and cried with me. Basically, they mobbed me and, like an ocean tide, carried me along with them to the game room.

There was such joy in that room, so many tears and so much laughter. I couldn't believe it. I was overwhelmed.

"We've been on strike," my friend Andy said. "We told them we wouldn't do anything—no meds, no food, no therapy, no sleep, nothing—until they brought you back. And they brought you back!" His face shone with triumph.

Andy felt—they all felt—empowered.

And I was beyond grateful. I was speechless.

One of the women there, Marilyn, who was about my mom's age, sat me down on the couch and wrapped me in her arms. I cried and cried and cried. I cried until I had no tears left. Everyone else stayed close to us, creating a protective circle.

I had no idea how much time had passed, but eventually one of the nurses asked if I would like to go to my room to get some sleep.

As a group, we paraded down the hall, walking shoulder to shoulder, until we arrived at my room. The other patients wanted to make certain no one took me away from them. When they saw me safely ensconced in my bed, they waved goodbye and got on with their daily activities.

I can only describe that moment and their actions—the way these people treated me—as a hint, a tiny glimpse, of heaven.

I had friends. Their compassion thawed my heart a little. I now understood not only that they cared about me but how much they cared. They cared to the point of going on strike for me, holding me in their arms, shedding their tears, and expressing their joy at my release. At the time, I didn't recognize the fullness of what they were showing me. These people, barely more than strangers, were my guardian angels.

Yet my soul and my body had been battered and beaten. Strangers loved me, but my heart kept repeating, *Your parents do not love you.*

Where would I go? What would I do? How could I ever face my parents again?

My family was not my family. My home was not my home.

The pain I experienced the night my parents returned me to the hospital—the physical, emotional, and spiritual pain—ate away at my heart. Had I not died a few months later at the age of sixteen, I doubt I would've survived my teenage years.

I kept asking myself, Was life worth the pain, the cost? Might it be easier to give up?

15

He Winked at Me

Later that afternoon, Dr. Kitts called me into his office.

I perched on the edge of my chair. I hadn't trusted him from the beginning. Now he terrified me. To me, he was the angel of death in the flesh.

He stood behind his desk. He seemed jovial, self-satisfied. This was the first time I'd seen him express any emotion.

He gave me a smug smile, as if we shared a secret. "How was your night?"

I remained silent. He knew exactly what my night had been like.

"What? You have nothing to say?"

"Why?" I asked. "Why did you do it?"

"Ah, well . . ." He dropped into his chair. "Works better than shock treatments to punish wayward teens. Don't you think?"

And he winked at me.

His words cut me to the core. They were downright cruel. The night had been horrible, abuse on top of abuse on top of abuse, the stuff of my nightmares. Yet his wink said it was all a joke to him. I wanted to throw up.

Perched on the edge of the chair, I couldn't keep my legs from shaking. The shaking spread to my entire body. I realized that this man sitting on the other side of the desk held all the power. And should he elect to use shock treatments or put me back in that locked unit, he would do so without hesitation and with the full cooperation of my parents.

A million thoughts raced through my mind. Thoughts like, *Doctors aren't supposed to do harm. Doctors don't punish patients.* Worse, my parents had given him permission to do whatever he wanted with me. They'd washed their hands of me.

My brain began to search desperately for a response. All those years of preparation for the Nazis came to the fore. I closed my trembling hands into tight fists, forced my legs to stop shaking.

"I won't run away again," I said. Somehow I managed to make my voice sound normal, reasonable. "You don't have to worry. I'm sorry I upset everyone."

"Well, we will see what happens."

There was a knock on the door.

"Yes?"

"Dr. Kitts, you have a phone call at the nurses' station."

He pushed away from his desk and walked past me without a glance, shutting the office door behind him, leaving me alone. I took advantage of the opportunity. I was desperate to know what was going on, what he had in store for me. I had to be quick. I leaned over the desk and flipped my chart around. I skimmed through the pages, looking for a plan of treatment, searching for any hints of what he might do next.

There was nothing. I didn't find a plan or any notes. Just doodles.

He'd been scribbling pictures during our visits.

I did see a diagnosis, which wasn't a diagnosis. It was a couple of sentences, a report from my parents: *Parents report patient exhibits defiance toward parental authority, is sexually promiscuous, sexually active with current boyfriend, has been sexually active with other adult males. Parents do not want her smoking cigarettes.*

I hurried to close the chart and turn it around to its original position so Dr. Kitts wouldn't know I'd read it. I sat back down in my chair, stunned. For one thing, Dr. Kitts had no plan of treatment, at least nothing I could find. For another, he had taken a side, and it wasn't mine. He wasn't my advocate. His intention was to make me compliant and agreeable, nothing more.

This wasn't therapy. I may have been only fifteen years old, but even I knew that. The issue I'd had with drugs, the reason I'd been willing to meet with a psychiatrist in the first place, didn't even merit a passing mention. I was floored by that omission. If my parents had provided Dr. Kitts with any information about my life or about my experience with the rabbi—and in my mind that was a big "if"—that, too, was absent from the chart.

The rabbi had repeatedly assaulted me for nearly a year. Another man, a twenty-four-year-old with whom I was barely acquainted, had brutally assaulted me just before I'd gotten together with Tyler, and that assault had also been set in motion by my parents' passivity and inaction.

That was the primary reason I'd gravitated to Tyler. He kept the bad guys away. Tyler had protected me when my parents had not.

Yes, I'd had a consensual relationship with my previous boyfriend, but I saw no mention of him in the chart. I certainly had never willingly had sex with other adult males, nor was my behavior in any way, shape, or form inappropriate or seductive. If anything, I went out of my way to go unnoticed.

There was only one explanation. Dr. Kitts's note confirmed for me what I had already known to be true. My parents blamed me, and he didn't question that. I was indeed the family scapegoat.

When I read those words, that purported diagnosis, it was as if someone ripped my heart out of my chest and stomped on it.

I was unloved and abandoned.

I was alone in the world. I was really, truly alone. Here and now, in this place, Dr. Kitts pulled all the strings. I couldn't count on the strength and friendship of the other patients, no matter how much they cared about me. Yes, they'd succeeded, or appeared to succeed, in helping me this time, but if Dr. Kitts and my parents decided to do something worse, no one would be able to stop them. Not even the nursing staff.

I sat there, my hands folded in my lap, staring down at nothing. I couldn't even cry. What would be the point of tears? My cause was lost. I was a lost cause. Dr. Kitts was correct. What I'd just experienced the previous night made a wayward teen compliant.

Dr. Kitts opened the door. "We're done here," he said. "I assume there will be no more incidents?"

"There will be no more incidents," I said. I walked out of his office, wishing I had died the night before.

———

I stayed in the psychiatric hospital another eleven days. I continued to spit out my pills, but my behavior was exemplary. I became the perfect patient. I participated in group therapy, extolling the virtues of my parents every chance I got. I agreed that my boyfriend was all wrong for me. Whatever had I seen in him? I painted, I played pool, I smiled if someone told a joke. I never once asked for a cigarette, nor did I make any phone calls or put in a request for visitors. I had none for the remainder of my stay. My parents neither called nor visited. I didn't see either of them until my discharge.

There was one thing I'd asked Dr. Kitts to ask of them. I'd made a single, albeit extraordinary, desperate request. It was my last hope. I'd discussed it with Dr. Kitts first, and he'd surprised me by agreeing. He'd broach the subject with my parents on my behalf.

I wanted to go to boarding school. I didn't want to live at home ever again.

When I'd put my request to Dr. Kitts, I was careful to leave my parents out of it. Instead, I said, "I think I'll have more discipline at boarding school, more structure. I think discipline would be good for me."

Dr. Kitts himself had attended a private Catholic boarding school. He'd told me all about it. He planned to send his oldest son to the same school. He was quite supportive of my idea.

My father came to pick me up. He met first with Dr. Kitts.

I waited in my room, my suitcase packed, my stomach churning. I had already said goodbye to my friends who were still in the unit.

My father walked through the door. I greeted him, and then I asked him if he'd discussed the idea of boarding school with Dr. Kitts.

"You're not going to boarding school," he said.

I took both his hands in mine and pleaded with him. "Please, Dad, please. Please let me go to boarding school. It would be best for everyone. I want to go to boarding school."

"You're not going to boarding school. We aren't paying money to send you away to school."

"Can we talk to Mom about it? Please?"

"Your mother has already said no."

I tried talking to my mother about it when I got home. She agreed with my father. I would not be going to boarding school.

And that was the end of that.

16

My Saving Grace

For the next few months, I went through the motions of living. I saw Dr. Kitts once a week and pretended all was well. Most of each visit, just as before, was spent talking about his children and his wife and her awful cooking. It would be a lie to say we spent more than a minute or two discussing my situation.

From time to time, he'd ask me, "So how are things?"

I would answer, "Fine."

We didn't discuss my hospitalization. We didn't discuss my drug use. We never once discussed my family.

I learned a lot about Dr. Kitts and his family. I learned a whole lot of stuff I didn't need to know. All in all, I came to consider him an acquaintance. I tried to view him as a neutral acquaintance. It was too painful and too dangerous to do otherwise. When it came to our interactions, I kept everything in neutral for my own safety.

I knew a great deal more about his life and his family and his unhappy marital situation than he knew about me. I felt as if I was his sounding board, his confidante. I was his patient, not his marriage counselor, yet the latter was often the role I played. That was inappropriate, yes, but I didn't object. Why rock the boat? If the man chose to hurt me, he could hurt me. I knew that now beyond a shadow of a doubt. I'd experienced his form of behavior modification once; I certainly had no desire to experience that kind of pain again. More than anything, I wanted to remain on his good side. I wasn't sure I could survive another encounter with his bad side.

When you get right down to it, if it hadn't been for my horse, Heather, I wouldn't have had any reason to live.

Of course, Dr. Kitts didn't know that. I never told him. He knew nothing about my interests and hobbies.

My father had received Heather in trade. He'd done some legal work for Charlie, who owned Shady Lane Ranch, nearly two years before my hospitalization. In exchange, Charlie had offered him a horse and had thrown in a year of free board and an old hackamore.

My father agreed, and the horse went to me. I loved horses. My dad had done a very nice thing for me.

Although I did a lot of babysitting around the neighborhood and worked as a waitress at a pizza place, I couldn't afford to buy a saddle. I needed the money for school clothes. It never occurred to me to ask my parents for the money to buy a saddle. Why would I? I knew their answer would be no. In their minds, a saddle would be a complete waste of money.

Riding bareback wasn't a problem for me. In fact, I preferred it. I had good balance, and I found riding bareback to be more comfortable and easier than dealing with a saddle. If I'd had a saddle on Heather when she fell on me, chances are I would have stayed dead. The saddle horn would probably have torn my aorta, lacerated my liver, or ruptured my spleen.

When I got Heather, Charlie had given me a choice between her and an older black gelding. I rode them both. I chose Heather because she was beautiful and fast. My parents weren't present that day, as it made no difference to them which horse I chose.

My sisters didn't ride, although my little sister occasionally climbed onto Heather's back and rode her around the barnyard or up the first hill. My middle sister was allergic to horses. And my parents had no interest in them.

Try as I might, I can't recall a single occasion when either of my parents saw my horse. My mother drove me out to the ranch from time to time, but I'm pretty sure she just dropped me off. I don't remember her ever entering the barn or waiting for me to retrieve Heather from the paddock so she could meet her. Neither my mother nor my father cared much for livestock kind of dirt, so they mostly avoided the ranch, although I believe my dad did see Heather once when Charlie moved her to another property a year or so after my accident.

My parents' lack of interest in Heather was my saving grace. She was the one thing I could call mine.

I'd been passionate about horses most of my life, and I'd done a lot of riding at Esther K. Newman Camp. I spent as much time with Heather as I could, riding her when the weather allowed, hanging out with her when the weather was lousy, just breathing in her comforting, earthy scent.

If I couldn't get a ride to the ranch, I walked the six miles or rode my bike, regardless of the weather. It didn't bother me. The only time I felt alive, safe, and at peace was when I was with my horse, riding her or grooming her. She was my one source of strength and love.

Every time I greeted Heather, I'd bury my face in her neck and inhale. There's something special about the smell of a horse. This is another thing I can't explain. It's almost as if the smell of my horse, the feel of my horse, kept me going. Heather was my one true friend. I had no need to pretend with her.

Ronald Reagan said, "There is something about the outside of a horse that is good for the inside of a man."* It's true. Heather was my best friend. She was my only close friend. I stayed alive so I could care for her, so I could ride her. When I was on my horse, no one judged me, abused me, or demanded that I comply with arbitrary rules. The only time I had any freedom was when I rode off into the hills.

After my discharge from the psychiatric hospital, I secretly resumed smoking. I met up with Tyler mostly during

*Ronald Reagan, "Camp David & Rancho del Cielo," Ronald Reagan Presidential Library and Museum, accessed November 16, 2023, https://www.reaganlibrary.gov/Permanent-exhibits/camp-david-rancho-del-cielo#:~:text=There's%20nothing%20better%20for%20the,10%2F10%2F1981.

school hours, but I was discreet, and Tyler was hurt by my refusal to be open about our relationship. I still saw my druggie friends, but again, I was cautious. After what I'd experienced in the hospital, I became even more secretive. Caution was my new rule of thumb. I no longer confided anything to anyone, not even my cousin Amy.

When I was home, I did as I was told. I completed all my chores. I was invariably polite and helpful, even when the requests and demands were inappropriate. I had no social life. I kept my nose buried in a book or listened to music. I pretended to do homework I'd already completed. I began cooking for myself as another way to control my calorie intake. I even took up bread baking. I didn't ask for anything. I rarely engaged in conversation. I spent most of my free time out at the ranch with my horse.

There were no more arguments with my parents. Since I made no requests, quit the dance team, attended no parties, and avoided social gatherings at school and after school, I had no reason to argue. Why should I? I barely had a reason to exist.

I still cared about my sisters and their welfare, and I helped them out when they needed help. I still cared about my grandmothers, my aunts and uncles, and my cousins. I adored animals. But I had no heart for myself. In my own eyes, I no longer mattered. I didn't see myself as a person worthy of any consideration at all. I accepted with all my heart what my father told me—my life had less significance than the tiniest, most microscopic speck of dust in this vast, infinite universe. That was me. Smaller than the tiniest, most microscopic speck of dust in this vast, infinite universe.

By nature, I'd been a kind, happy, optimistic, loving, caring, compassionate, and passionate child. I had a strong moral compass. I had good instincts about right and wrong. I had always believed that those traits were God's gifts to me because it seemed clear that love, happiness, hope, compassion, and a conscience hadn't been gifted by my parents. My parents weren't happy. They had no hope. And they didn't love me. At least, they didn't love me like a parent should love a child.

But at this juncture, none of that mattered. I dwelled in the shadows, pretending to be, as I always told Dr. Kitts, "fine," when in truth I was miserable. Outside of the time spent with my horse, I simply existed.

———

This was my state of being after what I'd experienced during my hospitalization and the years leading up to it. I was playing a part, nothing more. I was acting as though I cared whether I lived or died. But I didn't.

I've shared the sordid details of my story so you will understand that this was where I stood—how I viewed my life and life in general on the day I died.

God had saved me that horrible night in the hospital, but why? What was the point?

If there was a point, if there was any value in me as a person, I was blind to it. The will to live had been beaten out of me. I'd been released from the psychiatric hospital and admitted back into the asylum of my family. It was a familiar asylum, but now I saw it clearly for what it was, and unless I ran away from home and stayed away, I was trapped there. I did consider running away, but I didn't see the point. What would that accomplish? How would that make anything better?

I made no plans for my future because I saw no future for myself. I lived day-to-day, compliant, agreeable, moving like an automaton, without purpose aside from the time spent with my horse. Oh, I had improved my grades. I attended all my honors classes. I read loads of books and made films in my mass media class. I wasn't depressed. I wasn't contemplating suicide. But the truth was, I just didn't care anymore.

17

How Heaven Changed Me

In the months following my discharge from the hospital, riding my horse was about the only thing that brought me a sense of peace and healing. When I turned sixteen in April, I received my driver's license, so it was easier to get out to Shady Lane Ranch and ride Heather through the beautiful hills of western Iowa.

On the day of my journey to heaven and back, I was riding alone, which was just fine with me. I loved being alone with my horse. Despite all the pain and struggle in my life, I felt at peace.

When I heard the hoofbeats of that ill-tempered Arabian mare coming my way and had nowhere to go, I attempted to keep Heather under control. But she reared up and flipped over backward across my chest. At that moment, I died.

More than a few words need to be said here about the things Jesus told me as we surfed, about what I told others during my hospitalization after the accident, and about my thoughts and actions following my return to this life.

I returned a different person, a new person. I was no longer withdrawn. I no longer questioned my worth as a human being. I had been reborn, and I was more alive than I'd ever been.

I was still Jewish—yes, absolutely—but I was a different kind of Jew. I was a Jew who knew without a doubt that Jesus is who he says he is, that he *is* my Messiah. He *is* the promised, prophesied Jewish Messiah.

Did I have enough knowledge of Jewish Scripture to prove that point? I had none. I wasn't familiar enough with my own Jewish Scriptures to be able to pull out any sort of psalm, prophecy, or proof text. I was sixteen years old. It didn't occur to me to try.

I was familiar with Genesis, Exodus, some of Leviticus and Numbers, and Deuteronomy. I'd read Joshua, some of Judges, some of Kings. I loved the book of Ruth. It was my favorite book in the Bible. I'd read Esther. The only psalm I knew was Psalm 23, and that was because it was the psalm read at funerals I'd attended.

I knew nothing of the New Testament. As I mentioned, Tyler had given me a copy, but I'd never read it. At some point after my stay in the psychiatric hospital, it had disappeared.

But as I lay flat on my back in my hospital bed after meeting Jesus, none of that mattered. Jesus was the only thing that mattered to me, and I didn't know what to do with that. Who would believe me? Where would I go for answers? How would I piece together, make sense of, and come to terms with this marvelous, miraculous experience with God?

I went straight to God for answers. At long last I could talk to him. He was again what he had always been, my best friend, my Rock, and my Redeemer.

Boy, did I make up for lost time. As I lay in my hospital bed, I couldn't stop talking to God. And I didn't imagine or hallucinate my conversations with him because of any pain medication. I wasn't given any during my entire hospital stay.

Jesus and I had chatted and laughed all the way to God's lap. That I remembered. I couldn't remember everything he'd said, but I did remember this because he took his finger and wrote it on my heart: *All paths lead to truth, and all roads lead to God.*

That idea is controversial to Christians because Jesus said, "I am the way and the truth and the life. No one comes to the Father except through me" (John 14:6). But Jesus made it very clear to me exactly what he meant. When you die, there is only truth. Jesus is that truth. Truth in the sense of Jesus has a greater meaning, as in ultimate truth.

After death, we can't hide from the truth of our lives. Jesus sees it all. He knows it all. He knows everything about us. When we die, there are no more secrets. We will face the truth whether we like it or not. We can't hide from our words and deeds. We will face Jesus.

I can't speak for anyone else who has had a near-death experience. I can only tell you I saw the truth of Jesus, and with him I faced the truth of my own actions. Jesus is Truth with a capital "T." I loved him with all my heart. I accepted his infinite love, and I recognized what he had sacrificed for my sake.

I realized that Jesus loved me without any effort on my part. I hadn't done anything to earn his love. It was a free gift. His love was grace, undeserved grace. He showed me, of all people, undeserved grace. What a miracle!

Do all roads lead to God? Yes, in the end. This is what Jesus said to me. It's my understanding Scripture teaches that in the last days, we will all stand before God—all people, both the living and the dead—and we will face his judgment (2 Cor. 5:10; 1 Pet. 4:5). There's no escape from it. All roads, in the end, lead to God.

—

While Jesus was in my body with me, fixing me, repairing me, he left me with some final words of comfort. He said, "Your life is in good hands."

This caused me to experience immediate survivor guilt. "Why me?"

But he just smiled.

"Isn't everyone's life in good hands?" I asked. "What are they, chopped liver?"

Yes, I said that. Again, he just smiled. It was while studying his enigmatic smile that I realized what he meant.

Come good or bad, regardless of what happens in my life, I am in good hands. I am in his hands.

He was teaching me about faith.

136

"You die, you go to heaven with me, and you meet God," Jesus said. "Then you come back, and you live your life. Appreciate what I've given you. Be discerning, but try not to judge. Treat others the way you want to be treated."

He made it clear he didn't expect perfection. He told me to have children and be a good mother. But he expected me to follow him.

———

What does Jesus look like? I get this question often. It's natural to wonder how I saw him.

Jesus is totally human and totally divine, both at the same time. I have no way of explaining this, nor can I come up with better descriptive terms. He is a real person but a perfect person.

Jesus looks to be a man in his early thirties. He's around five feet ten and slender. He has wavy chestnut-brown hair with some lighter streaks that is almost down to his shoulders. Yes, Jews do have light hair. My father, for example, had white-blond hair and green eyes.

Jesus has a short beard and mustache. His face is long, and he has high cheekbones, deep-set eyes that turn up at the corners, and a strong brow line. His smile is wide and welcoming. His grin is infectious, his laugh contagious. He has straight white teeth.

His nose is long and thin but imperfect. It's perfect in its imperfection. I remember studying his crooked nose as he and I bodysurfed, thinking, *Someone must have broken his nose at some point. Maybe one of his brothers punched him in the nose.* This is odd because at the time of my death I didn't know he had brothers, nor was I aware he'd been beaten before he was crucified.

He has lovely hands and long, thin fingers. His feet, too, are long and thin. He has long toes.

He has beautiful, laughing, joyful eyes. They crinkle at the corners when he smiles.

I have no idea what I was wearing after I died. I only know I was wearing something and I was barefoot. To be honest, it didn't matter. Jesus was the only thing that mattered.

I've been asked if I saw any marks of the crucifixion on Jesus' wrists and ankles. I didn't see any, but his robe covered his wrists and ankles, so even if I'd looked, I couldn't have seen anything.

While I lay in my hospital bed twenty-four hours after my death, pondering everything in my heart, I knew I would go to Israel and walk where Jesus had walked, see the places he had seen. I would follow in his footsteps.

Even when I couldn't move, I believed I would walk again. There was no question in my mind. I didn't doubt it. Jesus gave me that confidence, that faith.

Jewish teenagers go to Israel all the time, but Jesus gave me a much more powerful reason to go. I needed to be near him. I knew I couldn't see him in person on this side of the grave, so I was determined to stand where he had stood, or at least as close to it as humanly possible. I would walk on the bones of my own Jewish history. And that history now included Jesus.

As you can imagine, in that hospital bed I had a lot of time to ponder. Jesus had made many things clear to me. I made some decisions.

My parents didn't come the first night of my hospitalization, but they did come to visit me the second night. After their initial greeting, they asked me how I was doing.

"I died," I said. "Jesus took me to heaven. I met God the Father. I sat on his lap. And then Jesus brought me back to my body."

I thought my dad might throw up. I had never seen anyone look so sick. He grew pale, turned, and left the hospital room.

My mother remained sitting at my bedside. She said, "We imagine a lot of things when we're hurt."

"I didn't imagine anything," I said. "I died. Jesus took me to heaven. I met God the Father. I sat on his lap. And then Jesus brought me back to my body. I told M about it right after it happened."

My mother looked uncomfortable but not completely disbelieving. She got up to leave, then stopped in the doorway. "Would you like Dr. Kitts to come talk with you?"

This was what I'd expected. But I was no longer angry or upset with my parents. Why should I be? I'd just spent an eternity with Jesus. I'd met God, my real Father.

"Sure," I said. "I'm happy to talk with Dr. Kitts. I'll tell him the same thing I just told you."

Dr. Kitts came to see me the next day. I told him exactly what I'd told my parents. He was silent for a few moments, then he said, "My wife made her awful carrot salad yesterday."

I laughed and asked, "So what else is new?"

Again, I wasn't angry or disappointed. I didn't expect him to believe me. As difficult as it is to believe, I no longer hated him and feared him for what he'd done to me in the psychiatric hospital. That was in the past, albeit the recent past, and I felt nothing but compassion for him.

———

The following day, our new rabbi came. This was a rabbi from the Reform Temple my parents had joined, and he was outspoken about his atheism. Like my father, he was proud of it. He sat down beside me, patted me on the shoulder, and said, "Tell me about this hallucination of yours."

"It wasn't a hallucination," I said. "I died. Jesus took me to heaven. I met God the Father. I sat on his lap, and then Jesus brought me back to my body. I can tell you more if you want to hear it."

He shook his head. "It was a hallucination. You had a hallucination while you were unconscious."

"I wasn't unconscious. I was dead. And being dead was the most real thing that's ever happened to me."

He got up and left the room. That was the last I saw of him.

18

A Blessing

The nurse who was most often on my floor happened to be passing by while I was with the rabbi. After he left, she peeked into my room. "May I come in?"

"Yes, of course," I said.

"I heard what you said—that you died, that you saw Jesus."

"Yes, I did."

"Please tell me what happened. I really want to hear about it."

Without hesitation, I told her everything. She not only believed me, but she also kissed me on my forehead and gave me what sounded like a blessing. She left the room with a big smile on her face. I guess she told a few other staff members because I began to get random visits from complete strangers, including the hospital priest. He seemed delighted by my description of Jesus. He stopped in to say hello every day after that, often sitting at my bedside for an hour or more. I appreciated his visits and his friendly face, as I had very few visitors during this long hospital stay.

What else did I do while I was in the hospital? Remember, Jesus had made things clear—in his way, not in a finger-pointing way. He didn't scold me. His way of communicating is heart-to-heart.

I called my friend Meryl, also an atheist like my father and our new rabbi, and I asked her to come visit. I told her my story.

She listened respectfully. When I reached the end, she said, "I don't believe in God. I don't know what happened to you, but God just isn't for me."

She left a short time later, after wishing me well. I reached out to her many times, not to preach but as her friend, only to be rebuffed. Her rejection didn't hurt my feelings; it wasn't personal, yet my heart ached for her sake. I hoped in vain that she would come back, renew our friendship, and talk to me about God. She never did. Tragically, she lived a sad, difficult life and died a premature death.

Tyler visited one evening, and I broke up with him on the spot. It was so hard, but I knew it was the right thing to do. Jesus had made it clear I'd been using Tyler as a crutch. He was my safety net. That was not supposed to be Tyler's role. I wasn't being fair to him or to his family. I didn't want to use him anymore. The entire episode with my parents had hurt him terribly, and my parents would never make amends, never accept him, never apologize, either to him or to his mother. He deserved better, and I knew he would ultimately make a much better match with someone other than me. I had a lot of healing to do, and I needed the time and the space to come to terms with what had happened to me, to learn how to live this new life. It wasn't the right time for me to have a boyfriend, and although I had male friends, I didn't date for a couple years following my accident. This was a time for me to focus on God.

Once I was released from the hospital after nearly a month, I managed my own recovery. My parents and I never spoke of my death. They avoided the subject. It was taboo. And I kept my mouth shut.

Once, I asked them if I could go to church. They said no.

I shrugged. It didn't matter. Church or no church, Jesus was still everything. In the meantime, I focused on healing, regaining the ability to walk, and finishing school.

———

I formulated a plan to graduate from high school a year early and leave for Israel. It would take all the money I'd saved over the years to follow through with this plan, but I didn't care. It would be money well spent.

I left for Israel at the age of seventeen. I studied Hebrew and worked on a kibbutz in the Lower Galilee, an hour south of the Sea of Galilee, forty minutes from the modern city of Nazareth. I hiked through the Upper and Lower Galilee and around the Sea of Galilee, all around the hills of Judea. I spent three weeks with a family near the historic village of Bethany. I spent as much time as I could in Jerusalem, which, in my opinion, may be the most special place on earth.

I stayed one night in the garden of Gethsemane. You could do that back then if you were sneaky. I just had to stay there. It was in that garden in the dark of night, leaning against an ancient olive tree, that I realized Christianity would have been stillborn without the resurrection. That's when the enormity of what Jesus had done for all of us hit me.

Because of his sacrifice, the kingdom of God had broken into this world. It was a hard concept for me, this kingdom of God, but there in the garden, I got it. The knowledge and understanding rushed through my body all in a single moment. It felt like the finger of God writing on my heart once again.

The next day I bought an English translation of the New Testament and read it for the first time. I was shocked to discover it was a totally Jewish book from cover to cover. I was perplexed. I asked myself, *How can anyone understand the New Testament if they aren't Jewish? How does it make sense if you aren't Jewish?*

I envied Christians. They not only studied the Hebrew Bible, but they also studied what seemed to be the rest of the Hebrew Bible. This collection of books, this New Testament, was my own heritage as a Jew, and it had been kept a secret from me. I'd remained ignorant. The "greatest hoax" in the history of humankind was my Messiah too. The revelation was shattering and heartbreaking but at the same time uplifting because I got it. I understood.

Yes, I'd met Jesus. Yes, he'd taken me to meet God the Father. I *knew* them. But I'd had no context for my

144

knowing. I'd had no context to correctly understand, interpret, and dissect everything Jesus had taught me. The New Testament in total provided the context, not only by relating the story of Jesus' ministry, his death on the cross, and his resurrection, but by pointing back to the books of the Hebrew Bible—the Torah, psalms, proverbs, prophets, and writings.

At long last I had a resource. It was reading the New Testament that inspired me to read the works of Moses, the Prophets, and the entirety of the writings in my own Hebrew Bible.

Israel was my heaven on earth. It still is. The very air I breathed, especially in Jerusalem, was different from anywhere else in the world. It's holy. It was living in Israel that healed me of my eating disorder. Because I had the freedom to make my own decisions; because happiness and joy weren't forbidden emotions; because God wasn't forbidden; because I had faith in myself, my surroundings, and God, I no longer needed to hold on to that lingering dysfunction.

After a year I returned to the States for three reasons. One, I missed Mexican food. You have no idea how much you miss Mexican food until you absolutely can't get it. I'm not joking. Mexican food is serious stuff!

Two, I knew if I didn't return home right then, I never would. Life in Israel, despite the dangers, was wonderful. I grew healthy, body and soul, in Israel. I was free there. Life with my parents would never be wonderful or healthy—that was clear to me—but I felt guilty staying away from my family for so long. Guilt had always been a major player in my life.

Three, the man I wanted to marry, the young man I'd met at summer camp when I was fourteen and he was sixteen, wasn't in Israel. If I didn't go home, he and I would never get married, and I knew clearly that he was my future husband. When the Holy Spirit speaks, it pays to listen.

19

Am I a Jew or a Christian?

My identity in Christ has been a struggle for me. Where do I, as a Jew, fit in? Although my friend and mentor Pastor John Burke is confident I have every reason to consider myself a Jew—a messianic Jew—I've recently been informed by two people, one a Christian and one a Jew, that I'm a Christian. This hits me where I live because I've straddled this fence for a long time.

I'm not sure how to respond to this. Perhaps no response is necessary. In all honesty, call me whatever you like. I don't care which label is stuck to my back. What people think of me is immaterial. What God thinks of me is everything.

I was born and raised a Jew in an orthodox community, and my mindset is that of a Jew. In other words, I think like a Jew. I always tell my Christian friends, "I don't speak Christian. I speak Jewish."

Yet I was told by my Jewish friend that I am not a Jew because I accept Jesus as the Jewish Messiah. She said I've turned away from Judaism. I've been told by my Christian friend that if I accept Jesus' divinity, then I am no longer Jewish. He says I've put my Judaism behind me. I am a Christian, period.

I haven't turned away from Judaism, nor have I put my Judaism behind me. I have turned back to the Jewish God, and I have put him and my Judaism before me. It is my very Jewishness and my own Hebrew Scriptures, on top of my experience with Jesus and his Holy Spirit after my death, that have helped me understand why Jesus is the Jewish Messiah. The Torah and the Writings, the Psalms and the Prophets, point to him. He is the living Torah.

I know in my heart my meeting with Jesus was true. He is the truest person I've ever met and ever will meet. He didn't tell me what to be in terms of labels. He told me what he *expected of me* in this life.

I was born of a Jewish mother and a Jewish father. We discovered through genetic testing that my father's bloodline extends all the way back to Aaron, the brother of Moses. My father carries the Aaron gene. According to Jewish law, I am a Jew. However, whether I'd legally be considered a Jew by Israeli law is another question. The answer is both no and yes. No because I've been baptized and therefore am considered to be a member of another religion. Yes because my father is Jewish, as is my grand-father and his father, all the way back to Aaron.

It's a weird place to stand. It's a kind of no-man's-land.

I'm not offended. To many Jews, Christianity has nothing in common with Judaism. What Christianity does have in their minds—what looms large in the Jewish psyche—is an unfortunate history of persecution at the hands of the church.

"Unfortunate" is an understatement, because we share a common beginning.

Jesus lived and died and was resurrected a Jew. He wore the mantle of Jewish messiahship. All his first disciples were Jews. They never thought of themselves as anything other than Jews. James, the brother of Jesus, took over as head of the Jerusalem assembly, or church, and he was revered by both Jesus Jews and non-Jesus Jews. The Jews who followed Jesus, including Paul, prayed, studied, taught, and discussed his words in synagogues. They followed Jewish dietary laws and the law of circumcision. But they were convinced the Law and the Prophets had been fulfilled in Jesus. And they believed in his resurrection. They knew what they'd seen. It was *real* real.

I had another epiphany as I sat in contemplation beneath that olive tree in the garden of Gethsemane as a teenager. Nobody with an ounce of sense dies for a lie. Almost all the earliest disciples died horrible deaths. Put yourself in their shoes (or sandals). Would you maintain such a lie in the face of extermination? I couldn't.

I would be heartbroken to lose my lifelong connection to the Jewish community. I cherish my relationship with Orthodox Judaism. My husband and I, along with our children and grandchildren, celebrate the Jewish holidays, and we keep kosher-ish in our home—no pork, no shellfish, no fish without scales, no mixing of milk and meat. We have separate dishes and cutlery for Passover but not for everyday use. We share meals with non-Jewish people. I don't cover my hair, and my husband wears a tallit and a yarmulke only on Shabbat and the holy days.

I'm also a part of a Christian community, one that accepts me as a Jewish person who believes in Jesus and all he represents. As a family, we celebrate Christmas, Easter, and Pentecost (Shavuot) in addition to other important Jewish festivals like Passover, Sukkot (the Feast of Tabernacles), Rosh Hashanah, the Jewish new year, and Yom Kippur (the Day of Atonement).

Community is everything to both Jews and Christians. I hope to continue to be a part of both. I'm an amalgam, but then, so were the first followers of Jesus.

Do I think Jesus renewed the covenant? Made a new covenant with us? Yes. Do I think that means all previous covenants with God were nullified? No. Rather, I believe all previous covenants have been or will be fulfilled. Jesus said that himself (Matt. 5:17–18).

God has a long memory, and he keeps his promises. He made a promise to our fathers Abraham, Isaac, and Jacob. He made a promise to the Jewish people at Sinai. He has kept and will keep his promises. Of that I am certain.

I like to quote Dr. N. T. Wright from his book *Paul and the Faithfulness of God*. Dr. Wright, who in my opinion is the greatest Christian scholar and apologist in my lifetime, states,

> Let us put it like this: to anyone who might say, "But, Paul, you are turning your back on everything Jewish; you are rejecting your own people; you are encouraging people to think that Jews are the wrong sort of people, that 'Judaism' (to call it that for the moment) is the wrong sort of religion," Paul would answer, "*mē genoito!* Absolutely not! I worship the God of Abraham, Isaac and Jacob; everything I say, do and think is rooted in Israel's scriptures; I celebrate the fulfillment of our national hope, the resurrection of the dead; I am a follower of the Jewish messiah, who (as our scriptures have taught us) is the lord of the whole world." This is a deeply Jewish position to take. To deny any scrap of this would be to take a step towards a non-Jewish or anti-Jewish stance, but Paul never moves his little toe an inch in that direction.*

I returned to life a born-again Jew, knowing with all my heart that Jesus is exactly who he says he is, the prophesied Jewish Messiah. There was and is no one else and nothing else to follow, only him. I am a sheep and I know the voice of my Shepherd.

Jesus says it far better than I ever could:

> What do you think? If a shepherd has a hundred sheep and one of them has gone astray, does he not leave the ninety-nine on the mountains and go in search of the one that went astray? And if he finds it, truly I tell you, he rejoices

---

*N. T. Wright, *Paul and the Faithfulness of God* (Minneapolis: Fortress Press, 2013), 542–43.

over it more than over the ninety-nine that never went astray. So it is not the will of your Father in heaven that one of these little ones should be lost. (Matt. 18:12–14)

And in Mark 2:13–17 we read,

Jesus went out again beside the sea; the whole crowd gathered around him, and he taught them. As he was walking along, he saw Levi son of Alphaeus sitting at the tax-collection station, and he said to him, "Follow me." And he got up and followed him.

And as he sat at dinner in Levi's house, many tax collectors and sinners were also sitting with Jesus and his disciples, for there were many who followed him. When the scribes of the Pharisees saw that he was eating with sinners and tax collectors, they said to his disciples, "Why does he eat with tax collectors and sinners?" When Jesus heard this, he said to them, "Those who are well have no need of a physician but those who are sick; I have not come to call the righteous but sinners."

20

God Is Love

Dying is the most real thing that's ever happened to me. It is *real* real.

Yet I appreciate the gift of this world. I love this earth. I won't neglect it, and I'm not in a hurry to leave it. I find it interesting that sometimes when people hear my testimony, they tell me, "I can't wait to get to heaven!" I respond, "Heaven is already here. God has a job for you right here. Don't be in such a hurry."

When God returned me to life, he didn't send me on a mission. He didn't instruct me to join a convent or become a missionary or a messianic rabbi. He simply gave me a second chance, a chance to keep my promise to him, a chance to get things right with myself and do my best to make them right for the next generation. I won't pass on the sins of my father. His pathological denial of God stopped with me.

As I've shared my story in various venues, I've met a few other people who've died as children and adolescents. It's interesting that many of us have one thing in common. We didn't return to life imbued with the notion that we, all by ourselves, could rescue the world. We didn't pick up that heavy burden and carry it on our frail shoulders. We're human. Without God's intervention, we can't save the world. I think one of the reasons we're dealing with so many issues today is because we're trying to do it all ourselves. We're leaving God out of the picture.

The simplest way I can describe this need for God is to say I learned that only he has such redemptive power. When a young person dies, they just sort of accept this truth. They accept the death experience. They accept what happened. The experiences a child has after death are loving. God and Jesus feel natural, normal. Jesus and God are home. Heaven is home. The young person realizes God is a part of them. He's a part of their life, the most important part. Jesus is a good friend, the best they can ever have. They come back grateful, amazed at Jesus' love and his sacrifice. Their head and heart aren't filled with worry and doubt, or at least, they worry less about the big picture. God has that in hand. He's got it. He's in charge. Even when it seems like things in our world are out of control, evil, crazy, completely messed up, that doesn't change. God is still in charge.

Jesus' basic message to me was simple. It was not necessarily easy to apply every single day, but at its heart, it was very simple: to love God with all your heart, soul, and mind, and to love your neighbor as yourself (Matt. 22:37–39).

I came back wanting to love, wanting to receive love. To love God with all my heart, all my soul, and all my strength. To love my brothers and sisters, knowing I don't have to like everything they do. To live my life as an example.

You get to take one thing with you in your heavenly suitcase. Not money. Not power. Not your house or your car. Not jewelry. Not awards or accolades. Not diplomas. Just one thing: love. The love you have for others, the love they have for you. That's it.

I'm no preacher, and believe me, I'm no better than anyone else. I'm not special. I'm not perfect. I'm not without sin—far from it. But God is all those things. He's special. He's perfect. He's sinless.

I also learned that, to paraphrase what we all said as kids, I'm not the boss of you. God is.

Jesus told me to be discerning but not judgmental. I'm not your judge. You are not mine. God is our judge. What I am, however, is accountable. I'm accountable for my actions and my words. One day I will face Jesus again, and I'd better be ready.

Jesus made it very clear that he doesn't deal in nonsense. He's honest and straightforward. He says what he means, and he means what he says. He's a down-to-earth kind of guy, the kind of guy you'd have a beer with. But he's also the kind of guy you'd follow to the ends of the earth.

I clearly understood that God keeps his promises. Our God is no fair-weather God. He's true and enduring. You can trust him with all your heart and all your soul. Above all, God is love.

Jesus is our Advocate, our Redeemer, our Savior, and our Messiah. He's God's human face because we cannot look upon the face of the Father, our Abba. Jesus is the Father donning skin and walking through life alongside us.

The Holy Spirit, in my experience, is Jesus' presence in our lives. I doubt I'll see Jesus again this side of death, but he left me with his presence. Jesus didn't make some big, fancy announcement about the Holy Spirit to me. The Holy Spirit just sort of manifested himself in my life. He just is. After I died and came back from heaven, I could feel him. I am never alone. From time to time things happen in my life that can happen only through the gift and the work of the Holy Spirit. He has a voice, and there's no mistaking it. I've heard it. When the Holy Spirit speaks, we will hear him. His voice is clear as a bell. Sometimes it's soft, but boy, is it clear.

God has a plan. We are living in that plan. My favorite religious studies professor said something that has stuck with me since college: "History is like a river flowing through time and space. The source of this river is God. A river cuts its own path, depending upon geography, weather, landscape, and time. Think of the Missouri River as it creates its own snakelike course, or the Colorado River cutting its way through rock, which has resulted in the Grand Canyon. But the river of history is directed by God, and from time to time, God sticks his finger in the flowing water, changing the course of history."

The birth and life, death and resurrection of Jesus was God sticking his finger into history big-time.

I believe the Bible is God-breathed. I believe in the resurrection, so you could say I believe in life after life after death. God will resurrect the dead; he will judge both the living and the dead. I've seen Sheol, the place where some of the dead sleep as they await God's judgment or redemption. Jesus held my hand and took me there. He said, "I have work to do, even here."

I learned there will be a new heaven and a new earth. What will that look like? I have no idea. Only God knows. The only thing I know is this: it will be good.

21

Dark, Existential Despair

It had been fifty years since my journey to heaven and back, yet the terror of death still drove my father. This terror was his sole motivating factor. For all of us, death represents the ultimate loss of control, but for my father, control was everything, he couldn't relinquish it, and this life was all he had.

Thus, in order to avoid dealing with this dark, existential despair, in order to avoid his fears, in order to avoid turning to God and faith for answers, he determinedly and deliberately shared his fears with others. He manipulated my mother, multiplying her own fear and anxiety and exacerbating her innate depression. She, in turn, lashed out at her children. My father manipulated us as well, forcing his fears upon us, blaming us when we couldn't assuage them, when we provided no solution, no cure, no alternative to death.

To a certain extent, my father achieved his goals. As a young child, I was desperate to please him, and I assimilated many of his fears, but ultimately, I rebelled. Even before I came to know Jesus many years ago, I rebelled against what I knew deep in my heart to be the wrong way.

Although I felt my father's fears, at the same time I sought solutions, escape. I sought refuge in God. It was after I died and met Jesus that I lost the fears that had been superimposed on me. This doesn't mean I lost all rational fear, but I no longer feared death. In fact, I was a hospice nurse for decades, providing comfort to people living their last days on this earth.

It's unfortunate that I can only describe what my parents did to me as a child as abuse—physical, emotional, and spiritual. I know it sounds trite, but my story is a bit of a maze, because the lives of human beings are a maze.

Humans are broken, but there is a fix for us. God has made it available to everyone, but he gives us a choice. We must want him, invite him into our lives of our own free will.

Even in old age, my father chose to remain broken. It was easier than facing his fears, and old habits die hard. When I first wrote these words, his doctor was referring him to hospice. That I was writing this book at the same time was the height of irony and tragedy.

Two months before his condition deteriorated and we requested hospice services, I planned a visit to my parents. God gave me a simple message for my father: *Look over your right shoulder. Here I am.*

My father wouldn't hear it. I tried so hard to convey the message. I struggled to find the right moment, but I realized there was no right moment. He didn't want to listen to me. He never wanted to hear about my NDE and my meeting with Jesus. He shut me down every single time I tried to discuss them, regardless of the words I used. I didn't push. I didn't intrude. I simply asked, "Do you want to talk about this? Are you willing to talk about it? May I tell you about my own death? Is there some way I can help you to feel less anxious and depressed?"

Death was anathema to him. Death was the enemy. For reasons unbeknownst to me, God was the enemy.

During my visit, I tried to speak with my father. I was met with silence and a dark stare filled with resentment.

After that time, God repeatedly reached out to my father. God graced him with visions of heaven and of hell. My father described these visions to us, and the hell he saw was exactly the hell I imagined for him, the one I always knew he feared. In his visions, he was alone for all eternity.

Yet my father chose hell every time. It was comfortable. It was familiar.

Visions of heaven frightened him.

As my sisters and I watched him suffer, we suffered right along with him. It was torture. It was heartbreaking. But my father made his choice long ago, and he was sticking with it. He wouldn't open his heart. He'd rather suffer than turn to God.

———

God always seemed logical to me, the only logical reason for existence. Nature fascinated me. The way I saw it, the beauty and the power of nature exemplified the mind of God. I observed animals, trees, and insects. I listened to birdsong and the squirrels' chirps and scolds. I marveled at the power of a galloping horse. I was thrilled by the roar of a lion. I was delighted by the sound of a babbling brook. I was awed by the beauty of a sunrise or a sunset, fascinated by the crackling of crunchy ice on a cold winter's day, and elated by a flash of lightning and the resulting crash of thunder. I couldn't imagine any reason for existence other than God. From my perspective, if there was no God, life made no sense whatsoever.

Why did I have an awareness of beauty? How did an awareness of beauty enhance evolutionary survival? If we were nothing more than evolved apes, as my father believed, what was the point of a sublime sunset, the glorious view of snow-capped mountains, or the soothing sound of gentle ocean waves breaking on a perfect white-sand beach?

In my opinion, God is the point. He, too, appreciates the beauty of the world he created.

I've studied evolution. I've considered the notion that perhaps food tastes good so that we will enjoy eating and thus eat to live. But why invent a food like pizza or French fries or aged stinky cheese? These foods are just frivolous when one considers evolution.

What about music? I suppose one could claim that music is a communal activity and communal activities improve survival rates, but then why make a Mozart? Wolfgang Amadeus Mozart was an unnecessary frivolity. What value was there in a Claude Monet? Or a Vincent van Gogh?

Why make a bluebird blue? What is the survival value of blue feathers?

What is the point of fun?

These questions and others confused me. I looked at nature and could not, for the life of me, understand why my parents said there was no God.

A conscience makes no sense if there is no God. Good behavior makes no sense. If there is no God, having a conscience is just plain useless. Selfish and self-centered behavior is far more effective for survival.

Why should I like someone or fall in love with one special person? Because that one person can best protect me and my offspring? No. I was convinced there had to be more to love than that.

Even cows have friends. It may not be obvious, but domestic animals like cows and horses have special friends, other animals whose company they prefer. Dogs do as well. If there is no God, then a special relationship, a bond, a shared understanding, or a good companion makes no sense. Those shouldn't matter. Only strength in numbers should matter.

Why should humans have any appreciation for the stars, wonder about the stars, or want to reach for the stars? There is no survival value in traveling into space. In fact, I think it's the opposite.

Does riding a roller coaster have survival value? Learning mathematics, physics, astronomy? What does literacy contribute to evolutionary survival? Think back to the most moving book you've read in your lifetime. How does storytelling, literature, the Bible, a novel, poetry, a biography, or nonfiction contribute to survival? Why would we learn to write?

Leaving anything for posterity is meaningless without a God and a hope for the future. Helping another person simply because that person needs help has no survival value.

Have you heard a robin's mournful cry when one of its babies is taken by a predator? I have. What that tells me is that even birds have enough self-awareness to understand loss and to mourn.

I've observed multiple species of birds join forces to attack a predator. Sure, that's survival, but it's something else too. It's cooperation. Under normal circumstances, robins, blackbirds, sparrows, finches, and wrens ignore each other, yet I've observed all these birds cooperate to go after a cat that was attacking a baby robin. It's not simply survival. Survival would mean letting the cat have the baby robin, not risking your short bird life to chase off a predator that is not coming after you or your offspring.

It was here that my parents and I most especially parted ways. I knew from a very young age that God existed. I wasn't sure how I knew; I just did. I knew he had existed forever—he'd existed before I was born, and he would exist after I died. I knew that he had created me and gifted me with consciousness and self-awareness, that he had created everything around me. He was beautiful and his creation was beautiful.

—

My dad suffered for months in hospice. His heart, which he'd feared his entire life would stop beating, just wouldn't stop beating. It pounded at two hundred beats per minute nonstop for nearly five days. How can the human body withstand such punishment, let alone a ninety-four-year-old man with severe right-sided and left-sided heart failure? He didn't suffer a stroke or a heart attack. He didn't rupture his aorta—which pounded as well—nor did he throw off a clot to his lungs and die of a pulmonary embolus. He'd lived in terror of those events throughout his life.

At the end of his life, when he desperately needed to die, none of these things happened.

God knew the reason. And we were about to find out why.

For a month or more I'd been hearing that my father wasn't long for this world. It would happen today. It would happen tonight. Maybe tomorrow.

Knowing my dad very well, I didn't drop everything to fly from my home in Montana to Oregon. He hung on, incredibly stubborn man that he was, clinging to life for all he was worth. He awoke from a hepatic coma to wander the hallways in his assisted living facility, saying things like, "I need to exercise more. I think my condition will improve if I just exercise more."

He'd say, "I think I'll live to be one hundred and five. Do I have enough money?"

He'd ask questions like, "Will this medicine reverse my condition?"

He simply couldn't make peace with his approaching death. He refused to talk about it. He wouldn't make plans for his funeral. He left us, his daughters, in limbo, struggling to figure out how to help him, how to comfort him, how to comfort our mother, and how to help her as she suffered with dementia.

He denied us that last gift of allowing us to give him un-conditional love. He couldn't make peace, so we couldn't make peace. His denial—or seeming denial—to come to terms with what was happening caused us terrible stress, frustration, sleepless nights, and heartache.

But a lot changed in the last thirty-six hours of his life.

22

"Dad, Jesus Will Be There, Waiting for You"

When I arrived and knelt at his bedside, my dad was semicomatose. He hadn't been able to speak clearly for twenty-four hours, aside from mumbling the occasional garbled word or name.

This was real now. My dad was dying.

I took his hand and kissed it. "Dad, it's Heidi. I'm here."

He opened his eyes and looked directly into mine. He grinned, a lopsided sort of half grin, half grimace. He took in my braids and said, "You look like a dog." Then he closed his eyes.

He didn't communicate again, aside from mumbling my sister's name or giving a slight nod or a hand squeeze.

One of my sisters was embarrassed for him, but his words didn't bother me. This was my father. His humor was often insulting, and I accepted that.

My father survived the night, barely. My youngest sister stayed with him.

I decided to stay in the apartment with him the next night. Did I want to be alone with him and my mother? If I was being honest, not especially.

But God pushed me to stay with him. I had to be there.

Earlier that day, my sister and I learned out of the blue, shocker of shockers, that our father had confided in one of his caregivers, a Christian who happened to be the pastor for her church's women's group. He'd talked to her about his fears, about God, about death, and about Jesus. He allowed her to pray for him and with him in Jesus' name, something she did regularly.

My sister and I were stunned.

I also learned that a man who had befriended my father over his last year was a pastor with a prison ministry. He's a pastor to two congregations in two different prisons. During my father's time in hospice, both prison congregations were praying for him. All my Christian friends around the country were praying for him as well.

During the dying process, my father never was open and honest with us about his thoughts and feelings, his fears and hopes. He declined all our efforts to help him find a rabbi, or any other member of the clergy, with whom he could speak to perhaps find some comfort. My father didn't want anyone Jewish to know he was searching for God. He didn't want anyone Jewish to know he was desperate for hope, for belief, and for heaven. After all, his lifelong reputation demanded a strict facade, an adherence to his brand of atheism, and the pretense that he needed nothing and no one. He certainly didn't need a crutch like that greatest of all hoaxes: Jesus.

Yet there he was, privately asking Christians to pray for him.

That night, after my sisters left, the apartment was quiet. I sat at my father's bedside.

My mother, despite suffering from dementia, appeared to be utterly engrossed in a day-old *Wall Street Journal*. I didn't know if she was reading it or simply staring at the page, but she said not a word, asked not a single question, which was very unusual for her as she tended to say the same thing or ask the same question repeatedly. Because she couldn't quite understand what was happening, she'd become increasingly agitated as my father drew closer to death. I was concerned that her agitation might affect his dying process. But for nearly two hours that evening, she remained uncharacteristically silent and still.

In the silence, I took my father's hand. "Dad, I forgive you."

He squeezed my hand.

I had forgiven him before, many times, but this time I held nothing back. I forgave him with all my heart.

"I'm sorry. I'm so sorry, Dad. I'm sorry I wasn't the daughter you wanted. I'm sorry I disappointed you. I'm sorry for every time I let you down."

Fair, unfair—it didn't matter to me. The truth is, I wasn't the devoted, compliant daughter he wanted. I couldn't help him with his worst fears. I'd failed him, and I needed his forgiveness as much as he did mine.

He squeezed my hand again, and he kept squeezing. I said the Lord's Prayer, and he tightened his grip.

> Our Father in heaven,
>   may your name be revered as holy.
>   May your kingdom come.
>   May your will be done
>   on earth as it is in heaven.
>   Give us today our daily bread.
>   And forgive us our debts,
>   as we also have forgiven our debtors.
>   And do not bring us to the time of trial,
>   but rescue us from the evil one. (Matt. 6:9–13)

I said the Shema, the holiest Jewish prayer, the prayer every Jew is supposed to say on their deathbed.

> Hear, O Israel: The LORD is our God, the LORD alone. You shall love the LORD your God with all your heart and with all your soul and with all your might. Keep these words that I am commanding you today in your heart. Recite them to your children and talk about them when you are at home and when you are away, when you lie down and when you rise. Bind them as a sign on your hand, fix them as an emblem on your forehead, and write them on the doorposts of your house and on your gates. (Deut. 6:4–9)

A tear slid from the corner of his eye. And I began to cry along with him.

I couldn't help it. I sobbed. But I managed to say, "Dad, when you die, look over your right shoulder. Jesus will be there, waiting for you. Accept his love, give him all your love. And give him all my love."

He squeezed my hand once more, and then his grip loosened. His breathing changed from labored to quiet and regular. He relaxed, and his respirations became more like soft sighs.

I closed my eyes and bent my head over his hand, tears streaming down my cheeks.

"Look at the light," my mom said.

I glanced at her and then looked around the room.

"The light just changed," she said.

She was right. My father had been surrounded by shadow, as if a gray cloud had hovered over him. Now all was bright—there was a brightness in the room. Yet the light, the twilight outside, hadn't changed at all. There was no sunshine pouring in through the sliding door, no window had suddenly appeared in a wall, yet it was as if someone had switched on a light.

The light emanated from my father.

Suddenly he lifted his legs and kicked out. It seemed to me that he kicked at something vile, like a poisonous snake. That's the only way I can describe his action. In all my years as a hospice nurse, I've never seen a dying patient do anything remotely like this.

I was stunned.

And then all was peaceful again. His face was relaxed. I knew he would soon be gone. I folded his hands across his chest and smoothed the wrinkles out of the sheet covering him.

I moved to the nearby table and opened my computer. A new video had been uploaded to a messianic Jewish

YouTube channel. It was a video discussion on Psalm 22, a psalm of David. It's about great suffering and the power of God's redemption, his power to redeem the sufferer. It's a prophetic psalm.

I kept the volume turned down, but I could tell my father was listening. Hearing is one of the last things to go.

When the podcast ended, I helped my mother to bed, well aware that when I returned to the living room, my father would be dead. Even my mother, despite her dementia, stopped at his bedside to say goodbye. She said, "He needs to go."

Twenty minutes later, when I came back to check on him, he was gone.

Shalom descended upon us. God had granted him shalom.

At last I could mourn him—mourn him like a true daughter, love him like a true daughter. I felt a rush of grief mixed with joy. Grief because my father had suffered, because we had both suffered, not just now, not just with his death, but our entire lives. Joy because God had gifted my father with time—the time he needed to turn to him.

23

God Took Care of Me

Several years before she developed dementia, my mother sat down beside me on the couch. She said, "I want to apologize."

"For what?" I asked.

"When you were fifteen, you were invited to a party. It was a special party. Do you remember?"

Oh, that. I nodded. *Yes, I remember.*

"You were so excited about this party. You spent hours choosing the right outfit, doing your hair. And when you were dressed you looked so pretty. You came downstairs singing. You were glowing with happiness, because for once I had said yes."

"I remember."

"And then, when you were waiting for a ride to the party, I got scared. I didn't want you to go. I knew there would be parents there to chaperone, but still, I was afraid to let you go. So as you stood there, hopeful, waiting, smiling, I said, 'You're not going to the party. Go change your clothes.'"

"Yes, I remember that too."

"You burst into tears. You ran up to your room. I knew I had hurt you. You'd been so happy. You'd been singing all day, looking forward to this party. You were sobbing, and I felt bad, so I went upstairs and opened the door to your room, and I told you that you could go to the party. You jumped up, so happy, so thrilled, and you hugged me. You dried your eyes, fixed your hair, and ran downstairs and waited for me to drive you to the party.

"But I got scared again. I came downstairs and told you I'd changed my mind, that you couldn't go to the party. You just looked at me, confused. 'You can't go,' I said. 'I've decided you can't go.'

"You said you hated me, and you ran up to your room and cried. So I came back upstairs, and I told you that you could go. You looked at me, not sure you could trust me, but I said, 'Yes, you can go. I'll drive you.'

"You came downstairs again. You'd fixed your hair and tried to soothe your puffy eyes. You weren't happy and smiling this time. You looked doubtful. And then I did the worst thing I could do. I told you that you couldn't go.

"You cried all night. I know. I could hear you crying. I don't know why I did that."

I was speechless. Of course I remembered that day. It was typical of our interactions during my teenage years. This incident had been especially painful and confusing.

"I didn't know how to raise a teenager," she said. "My mother didn't really raise me. I was raised by the help. I didn't know how to be a mother to a teenager, and I was scared."

"What scared you, Mom?"

"I don't know. I was just scared, so I didn't let you do the things your friends did. I don't know why I acted like that. I'm sorry. You were so happy that day, and I ruined everything for no reason. I'm sorry."

"Thank you for the apology, Mom. I'm sorry I said I hated you."

———

Before my mother's dementia worsened, she asked me several times about my NDE. She asked me about Jesus. She always prefaced any discussion by asking about Charlie, the owner of Shady Lane Ranch—the site of my death—but this was a code. What she wanted to know about was my meeting with God.

Prior to her dementia, she didn't allow herself to ask. Our only discussion of the accident was forty-eight hours later as I lay in the hospital bed. It was a one-off. We didn't discuss my death again. But in a strange and marvelous way, God blessed her. She no longer remembered this was a taboo subject.

My mother couldn't recall everything, but for someone with dementia, her long-term memory remained remarkably intact, at least until the past few years.

Our conversations about my accident and God unfolded like this:

"Weren't you in a bad horseback riding accident?" she asked.

"Yes, Mom, I was."

"Didn't Charlie find you?"

"Yes, it was Charlie who picked me up."

"Do you think he's still alive?"

"I don't know."

"Do you think he still owns Shady Lane?"

"I don't know."

I saw her turn inward, scrolling slowly through her memory files. "Did you die in that accident?"

"Yes, I did."

"Did you go to heaven and see God? You saw Jesus, didn't you?"

"Yes."

"That's good. I'm glad Jesus was there for you. That was a terrible accident. Why didn't we take care of you? I don't remember taking care of you. We sent you to that bad hospital, that other hospital, didn't we?"

"It's okay, Mom. God took care of me."

She shook her head. "I wasn't a very good mother."

"It's okay, Mom. I'm fine."

"You're a good mother," she said. "I'm glad you're a good mother. I always wanted to be a good mother. I don't know what happened to me."

My tears flowed. I put a hand on her arm. I would have hugged her, but she didn't like displays of affection.

I know what happened to her. My father happened to her. My mother, who was born into a family with many members suffering from chronic depression and was already prone to severe bouts of depression and anxiety herself, had no time or energy left for her children. My father required all her energy. We children were a burden.

24

Surrounded by Angels

I've always envied those who have a loving relationship with a parent or parents, especially a loving, supportive relationship with their mother. There's something so marvelous about the love between a mother and child. I've experienced this with my own children and grandchildren. Our interactions aren't without disagreement, though. When my children were teenagers, there was plenty of yelling. On rare occasions even now, we exchange angry or critical words, but we love and support and forgive each other through thick and thin. Children are God's greatest gift to humankind, one step down from his own Son.

If there was one thing I learned when I was dead, it was this: God loves children. They are lifted directly into his arms.

I never experienced this sort of close, loving relationship with my mother, so the conflict in my heart was all the greater. It was hard to reconcile the end of her life.

I couldn't say, "Oh, but she had such a wonderful life! She and I shared such joy! At least I'll be left with a treasure trove of precious memories." In truth, I couldn't say I would miss her loving presence in my daily life. But I could say I would miss her, I would remember her, and I was grateful for the things she taught me.

God knows just how much I wish things were different.

I never wanted to be responsible for my parents. Yet here I was, caught up in the irony once again, responsible for the mother who didn't always want to be responsible for me.

Let me tell you, God knows exactly what we need. It may not be what we want, but it's what we need. And he reminded me of that a mere six months after my father's death.

As I sat by my mother's side, I couldn't help but think of Jesus' words when I was in heaven: "You have to go back." He had his reasons.

After my father died, our family moved my mother from Oregon, where my parents had lived after my father retired, to a memory care facility ten minutes from our home in Montana. She'd been receiving hospice services for a couple months, but just before New Year's 2023, to our utter dismay, she was discharged from hospice. She didn't qualify based on a diagnosis of dementia. I prayed—oh, how I prayed—that she could soon be readmitted to hospice because both she and I needed the help and support.

On New Year's Eve, I came down with influenza. I felt as if I'd been hit by a truck—fever, aches, chills, a sore throat, and a cough. One hour I was fine, nibbling on hors d'oeuvres, the next I was flat on my back in bed.

A little over forty-eight hours later, the phone rang. It was 2:00 a.m. and I stumbled out of bed, not even sure where I was. The med tech from my mom's memory care facility was calling. My mother was experiencing chest pain and shortness of breath. Because she was no longer a hospice patient, the med tech had no medications to give her to ease her symptoms. Her vitals were stable, but she was very uncomfortable.

The staff and I went back and forth for a couple hours. At 4:00 a.m. I asked them to send her to the emergency room because her condition hadn't improved. Although they had done what they could with the medications at their disposal, they had no way to manage her symptoms and hadn't yet heard back from her physician.

Once a doctor was able to order tests and examine her, my mother came out of the examination with three terminal diagnoses. She was dying, fast. She returned to the facility—the staff of memory care was kind enough to send a shuttle to pick her up—and she was immediately readmitted to hospice.

I wasn't sure when my mom would arrive back at the facility, but I knew I had to be there to meet her. I'd do my best not to infect anyone else, but it was clear my mom wasn't long for this world. I needed to be with her.

I entered through the back door, avoiding contact with everyone, and walked straight to her room. I was surprised to see her sitting in her wheelchair, perfectly serene like the subject of a Renaissance painting, hands folded in her lap, bathed in a golden light.

She was surrounded by angels.

Even when I died, I didn't see angels. And now I saw eight of them standing in a circle around my mom. I stopped in my tracks. I didn't know what to do. Should I look at them? Should I look away? Should I fall on my knees? I wondered if I should remove my shoes because this was holy ground.

I wasn't afraid, but I was frozen in place.

They turned to me, all of them at once. They gazed at me, their expressions unreadable. These tall, beautiful angels were there for my mother, for her alone. Yet they had granted me the privilege of seeing them.

My mother lifted her head. "Heidi, I'm so glad you're here."

And with those words, I was essentially allowed into their holy presence.

My mother's voice was calm and tranquil. The ever-present anxiety, agitation, irritation, confusion, fear, anger, pain, longing, regret, and sadness I'd come to expect had vanished. She looked beautiful; her skin glowed with youth. She was alive, yes, but it was clear she'd already crossed the threshold. She had already spent time with God.

She didn't waste a second. "I want to be buried beside your father in Oregon. How do I make those arrangements?"

"I've taken care of it, Mom. Your plot is right next to Dad's. I've made all the arrangements to have you flown back home."

She smiled. "Thank you."

"You're welcome."

In some families, this would've been a hugging moment. But it wasn't for us. Over my lifetime I'd learned to respect my mother's need for space. We sat together and that was okay.

"Are you in pain, Mom?"

She shook her head. "Not much. You know, last night when I was in so much pain, my oldest friend was with me."

"Oldest friend?"

"You know, my oldest friend."

I didn't know if she meant Mary, a friend she had made in memory care, if she meant a friend from childhood, or if she simply referred to an old person.

"Who, Mom? Who was with you?"

"My oldest friend. She told me everything would be all right. She stayed with me."

"Was it Mary, your friend here?"

"No, of course not."

"Was it the staff? I know they were here."

"No, it wasn't the staff."

I tried to think of everyone she had ever known—family members and friends, living and dead—whom she'd mentioned to me during my lifetime. I named person after person. She shook her head after every single name.

I did forget one name, Blanche, her oldest and best childhood friend. My sister told me to ask about Blanche, yet when I said the name, Mom shook her head again, although she did describe Blanche as her best childhood friend.

For an hour, as the angels looked on, I had my mother back. Her mind was clear, her memories restored. We chatted about everyone and everything in her life. We talked about the living and the dead. We laughed. We cried. She was my mom, and she was so beautiful.

But she grew weary, and her pain increased. The hospice nurse and I helped her into bed.

The next day, my husband and our oldest daughter, Jennie, came to say goodbye. My mother was sleepy, but again, her mind was clear. She was so happy to see the three of us. She asked about her great-grandchildren. She asked about Jennie's rancher husband.

Then, out of the blue, she looked right at me, gave me a little smile, and said, "Do you think Charlie is still alive?" There was mischief in her voice and a twinkle in her eyes. "Is Shady Lane Ranch still open?"

And I knew right then she had met Jesus.

Those two questions were the code she'd always used when she wanted to talk about what I witnessed in heaven. Jennie and I exchanged glances.

My mom gave me a wink and a nod. My eyes filled with tears.

My mom soon grew tired, and we said goodbye.

She said, "Have fun. You should have fun. I never had fun in my entire life." She closed her eyes and whispered, "Life is meant to be fun."

After that, she slept for ten days with her arms folded across her chest. She rubbed her nose on occasion and groaned rarely, but she never woke up again. She died the most peaceful death I have ever witnessed, and I've seen a whole lot of death.

I had a dream the night my mom died. In my dream I entered her room. There was a party going on. Many of her dead relatives and friends were there, dancing and singing. My mother was dancing. She was really shaking her booty. She was having so much fun.

Suddenly the wall to the outdoors vanished, and I saw a train waiting to take her to heaven. Everyone at the party walked right through the side of the building and got on that train. My mother waved once, and she was gone.

I was awakened from that dream by a phone call from the memory care facility. My mother had just passed away.

The angels had taken her home to heaven.

Who was her oldest friend, the person she'd seen the night she suffered so?

I guess I'll find out one of these days. Could it have been Jesus? It wouldn't surprise me.

My mother was beloved by so many relatives and friends, and I'm glad of it. She didn't love me with her whole heart, but she loved me enough.

Within a span of six months, the two people who at times were my greatest adversaries, the two people against whom I often defined myself, were gone. So much of my life was spent trying to love them, trying to earn their love. On my own, I failed. My parents and I set store by different treasures. That changed at the very end when everything fell away, and all was forgiven.

My mother was right. Life isn't meant to be sad, angry, and hate filled. Life is meant to be fun. It's too late for a do-over for our family; what's done is done. Nevertheless, I'm as grateful as grateful can be because nothing is ever too late for God's family.

My father was like the prodigal son. He ran off and squandered all he had been given. When he returned to his Father, I know for sure there was great rejoicing in heaven.

My mother was more like a lamp hidden beneath a bed. At times her light shone for all to see, but most of the time it remained hidden. At the end of her life, there it was, shining bright, clear as day—the light, the angels, and the love.

25

A Dream or a Vision?

Smack-dab in the middle of rewriting this book, I had a dream about my friend, pastor and author John Burke. In my dream, he insisted upon meeting Jesus. He just had to meet him, had to see him in person, had to know the man Jesus and the Lord Jesus. John begged and begged me to take him to paradise so he could meet him.

Reluctantly, I agreed. "Jesus may not be what you think," I said. "He's not exactly what you expect."

"I don't care," John said. "I have to meet him."

In my dream I totally understood his burning desire to meet our Lord and Savior. John has spent decades listening to stories of NDEs, and now he's working on a new book about NDEs. He wanted to meet Jesus for himself.

So in my dream, off we went to paradise. We found ourselves standing before a vast hall made of huge, smooth, glowing white stones. We walked beneath an arched gateway into the hall. There on the floor sat countless people—adults and children—all waiting patiently for Jesus. Beyond the crowd was a long stone staircase curving away, leading up and up, the top of the staircase well beyond our view.

John and I stood respectfully off to the side, but he was hopping about, so filled with anticipation and joy that he couldn't stand still. And here they came, descending the stairs, the sages and the saints from all time periods. I recognized St. Augustine, St. Philip, the prophet Jeremiah, St. Paul, even the prophet Habakkuk. I don't know how, but I knew them all, at least by sight. Each sage, each saint, each patriarch was dressed in garb appropriate for his own time. They descended the massive staircase in groups, their heads together, discussing matters of great import. Silent, the crowd watched them pass—recognition, respect, and reverence in their eyes and demeanor.

"Is that him? Is that him?" John pointed out one man after another as they passed us.

"No," I said. "He's not what you think."

"But one of these men must be him."

I shook my head. "Be patient. He will come."

And he did. I recognized him instantly. Jesus descended the stairs last, a humble man, nondescript, dressed in a humble robe, wearing a worn tallit over his head and shoulders. He didn't pass us and leave through the doorway as the sages and saints had done. Instead, he grinned and walked over to the waiting crowd. He sat down cross-legged on the floor in their midst. In a heartbeat he was surrounded by children climbing all over him, sitting on his lap. He pulled his tallit over his face and played peeka-boo with the littlest children. He made funny faces at the older children. Everyone laughed, overjoyed to be in his presence.

I forgot all about John. I ran to Jesus and hurled myself at him, propriety gone. Jesus caught me, steadied me, and helped me to stand, and I realized all I had done. I collapsed into a puddle of tears at his feet, heartsick.

He knelt, but I couldn't lift my head, couldn't look him in the eye.

He asked me, "Why do you cry?"

"All the missed opportunities!" I was sobbing now. "You've given me so many opportunities, and I've squandered them."

Jesus lifted my head with his hands. He smiled at me. "You know what to do. Go back and do it."

Suddenly I remembered John. Jesus turned and looked at him. "He's my good friend," he said.

And with those words, John and I were back on earth.

"Do you see?" I asked. "He's not what you expect. He's first but he's last. He doesn't leave with the saints and the sages; he plays with the children. He's humble and human—the very most human human being in the entire universe."

But John didn't answer. He couldn't speak. He was sobbing.

And then I awoke.

Imagine God's plan as a circle, but his circle is infinite in size. Within this circle, we take our steps, we make our choices, and we exercise our free will, but all our choices are contained within this circle, within his plan. Our human eyes can't see his plan; our human hearts can't even imagine his plan, yet it exists. I trust Jesus, the very most human human being in the entire universe, and I hold tight to the words he spoke: "Your life is in good hands."

> I trust in you, O LORD;
>   I say, "You are my God."
> My times are in your hand. (Ps. 31:14–15)

Afterword

I am Heidi's sister. Her account of these events is true. The story she tells is not only about life's challenges, but most importantly, it's about the power of forgiveness to heal, repair, and make whole again. Heidi and I have both had to learn the lesson of forgiveness many times in our lives.

Not only do I recall my sister's horseback riding accident, but some of my experiences paralleled hers. I too had unfortunate encounters with the rabbi and with Dr. Kitts.

I was ten years old during Heidi's bat mitzvah year. Although she didn't give me any details, Heidi warned me several times to stay away from the rabbi, to not be alone with him, and to never allow him to touch me or kiss me. Unfortunately, I couldn't always avoid him. He'd grab me and pinch my cheeks so hard it made me cry.

I was at the synagogue for after-school Hebrew class when the rabbi instructed the students to troop down to the basement sanctuary to practice the readings and Hebrew prayers as they would be done in a Sabbath service.

He stood in the center aisle close to the front of the sanctuary, with the students sitting in chairs in rows on each side. He asked a girlfriend of mine and me to help with the reading of the Hebrew prayers. She stood to his left side, and I stood to his right. The rabbi put his hand across my back, reaching all the way to my right shoulder. He had his other hand on my friend's back. I was in the middle of reading a prayer when I felt the rabbi's hand slide under the neck of my shirt, down my upper chest. His fingers slid down into my training bra.

I immediately threw my siddur to the floor and shouted to my friend, "Run!" We raced away toward the girls' bathroom. When we reached it, I told her what the rabbi had done. We snuck into the kitchen to use the wall phone there. I called my mom and begged her to come pick us up, then my friend and I waited outside for her. I don't think the rabbi was planning on my response. I didn't care what any of the other kids thought. My goal was to stop him and escape.

When we arrived home, my mother and father called me into the living room. My mom sat on the couch, my dad in his reading chair. Heidi came downstairs and stood near me. I told my parents what had happened. I tried my best to convince them that I was telling the truth. I remember my mother saying, "He's your rabbi. He wouldn't do that," and my father saying, "Your mother is right about that." I remember how upset I was. I was in tears and kept saying, "But he did. He did it." Heidi spoke up, saying, "Yes, he would do that."

But nothing changed. He remained our rabbi, and I avoided him as much as possible.

I remember Heidi's accident a few years later. It was very shocking and traumatic for all of us. I was in the car waiting for Heidi to finish her ride. Because of my allergies to horses, I tried to stay away from the dust and dander and often took some breaks in the car when I was at the ranch.

I saw Heidi return. She had stopped and was sitting on Heather near the corral, on a small rise, kind of facing the car and the parking area. Suddenly a man flew down the hill on a horse, racing out of control at a gallop toward the barn. His horse was extremely close to Heidi and Heather, and from my vantage point, it looked like the horse was going to slam into them.

Heather reared up as Heidi tried to hold on. Then Heather reared up and back so far that Heidi flew off and hit the ground hard, and Heather fell over backward, with her full body landing hard over my sister's entire midsection. Heather rolled over Heidi and got to her feet, then ran straight into the barn. Heidi was just lying on the ground and looked unconscious or dead.

I was in shock and frozen for a moment. My little sister began sobbing and screaming, "She's dead, she's dead!" I got out of the car and both of us ran up to Heidi.

Shortly afterward, Charlie quickly came out of the barn with Heather. After maybe five minutes, Heidi roused, opened an eye, and said something. Charlie brought Heather to her and somehow lifted Heidi to put her back on the horse. Heidi was totally limp. I was still in shock, thinking, *Why doesn't someone call an ambulance? Why is Charlie putting her back on the horse?*

I rode in the car with Heidi lying in the back. Charlie drove us home and carried her up to her bed. I heard that the next day Heidi had to crawl downstairs with her arms so my mom could take her to a clinic. I never went to see her at the hospital. I don't know why nobody took me to visit her. I don't think any of us went to see her aside from my mom, when Heidi called home to say she needed help because there weren't enough staff at the hospital.

My mom and dad didn't really talk about Heidi's accident. I only remember they said Heidi was in the hospital with a broken pelvis. When she finally came home, she used crutches for a long time. I honestly don't remember my parents saying much about the situation at all.

———

I used drugs recreationally during high school. It was nothing serious—a social thing at weekend parties. Like Heidi, I didn't really like drugs. Unlike Heidi, I did my best to never let my parents know what my friends and I were up to.

Once I entered college during the quiet summer session, things were going well, but in the fall, masses of students returned, including many of my friends. There was much pressure to be part of a social group. My all-girls dorm was wild with weekend parties, alcohol, and drug use. I began to feel lost.

One Saturday night I went with friends to a bar in downtown Iowa City to hear live music. I was sitting at a small table with four others, drinking beer, which I really disliked, but I drank to fit in with my group. At some point, maybe by my second beer, someone handed out some white tablets, with no clear definition of what they were. Having already smoked quite a bit of pot before we arrived, I joined in, washing the small tablet down with my next swig of beer.

Soon everything felt off. I felt sick and mentally unclear as I tried to figure out what was happening around me. I don't know what those white tablets were, but I spent most of the night vomiting and by morning I was a wreck. I became seriously depressed for weeks afterward. I felt that my social life and weekend habits were dimming my clarity, seriously disturbing my body, mind, and spirit. I no longer kept up with my courses, which was not normal for me. I felt finished with university life, with the sense of emptiness, and especially with the drug culture I'd dabbled in since the tenth grade. I called my parents and told them I needed to quit school and come home. They came and picked me up, but they were not happy about me leaving school.

Once home, I felt more depressed than ever and shared that with my parents. It was a combination of having no sense of what I wanted to do with my life, as well as feeling I'd never been seen, as if I was invisible. I was expected to step into the adult world with no preparation. I couldn't find my footing. I found myself depressed and crying much of the time. My parents told me they wanted me to see a psychiatrist they knew, a doctor they had sent Heidi to see in her midteens. My parents talked about Dr. Kitts as though he was God. They said, "Dr. Kitts will be able to help you."

With little insight into myself and my needs and parents who had no clue about who I was or what I needed, I agreed to see Dr. Kitts. I sat in his office for my first appointment, Dr. Kitts swiveling in his big chair behind a massive wood desk. He asked me to tell him what was going on. I shared what had happened at college with drug use and drinking, and how that environment seemed to send me into a depression. He didn't ask me any more questions. He didn't use our session to connect with me and get some sense of what might be going on and what might be helpful, though he was quite eager to immediately write me a prescription for a medication that turned out to be a strong tranquilizer.

That same day I took the first shiny, dark green pill. The instructions were to take one or two a day or as needed. After the first dose I was knocked out, feeling heavily drugged. After the second dose I stopped. The next week my parents sent me back to Dr. Kitts, and he asked how things were going with the medication. That was all he asked. That was all he was interested in. I told him the pills made me feel like a zombie and I had stopped taking them after the second dose.

To my parents' disappointment, I refused to see Dr. Kitts again. On the bright side, I stopped using drugs and alcohol when I made the connection between how they affected my nervous system, mind, body, and emotional state. That was a needed and welcome lifelong change for me. The entire experience was a catalyst launching me in a new and positive direction. Not long after, I moved across the country, beginning a positive transition into my adulthood.

Although our life experiences in total may have been very different, as children and teens and even young adults, Heidi and I experienced much in common. We lived through many storms together and separately. Some were navigated with dignity and compassion, and others not so much.

In our relationship, Heidi and I have both said and done things we have regretted, but always we found our way back to one another. I am a practicing Jew and not a messianic Jew as she is. For decades I studied teachings from the world's religions, including Christianity and the teachings of Jesus, Islam, Buddhism, and Hinduism. I know about Heidi's near-death experience and relationship with Jesus. I honor her experiences. She has shared her personal choices with me for years.

After our father died in 2022, we both worked painfully hard to maintain and repair our relationship in the face of serious challenges. Through our sessions together with a forgiveness educator, we have truly found a solid and loving sisterhood. We've come to trust each other and to cherish one another. We both agree that it is through the grace of God that we not only survived our challenges but have also thrived.

Sari Telpner
Credentialed Health Educator and
Certified Nature and Forest Therapy Guide

Acknowledgments

I wish to acknowledge the following people. Some contributed with their steadfast encouragement, some with their steadfast love, and some with both.

My husband waited for me to come around. Then he came around. He is the love of my life.

My children and my grandchildren fill my heart with warmth, joy, worry (I am a mom, after all), and most of all, love. They are gracious gifts from God.

Pastor Bob Schwahn patiently listened to my story without even knowing me. He was concerned I might tell him a crazy tale of alien abduction. He listened anyway. He and his wife, Carmen, have become our dearest friends.

Pastor John Burke, author of *Imagine Heaven*, has been my muse. He's encouraged me and supported me in my journey. He's been behind me all the way. It was he who told me it was okay to be Jewish.

Last but not least, every single ounce of gratitude I have goes to my Lord and Savior, Yeshua. He answered my prayers.

Heidi Barr, a Jewish girl who once had nothing to do with Jesus, died and met him as a teenager. Now she's a former hospice nurse living with her husband in Bozeman, Montana. Learn more at her website, NewHeaven.biz, or find her on Amazon.